Dealing with Demanding Customers

■

This book is to be returned on or before

7/10 cw

114010

LLYFRGELL
LEG MEIRION DWYFOR
LIBRARY

The Institute of Management (IM) is at the forefront of management development and best management practice. The Institute embraces all levels of management from students to chief executives. It provides a unique portfolio of services for all managers, enabling them to develop skills and achieve management excellence. If you would like to hear more about the benefits of membership, please write to Department P, Institute of Management, Cottingham Road, Corby NN17 1TT. This series is commissioned by the Institute of Management Foundation.

Dealing with Demanding Customers

How to turn Complaints into Opportunities

■

DAVID M. MARTIN

in *the Institute of Management*

FOUNDATION

PITMAN PUBLISHING

Pitman Publishing
128 Long Acre, London WC2E 9AN

A Division of Longman Group Limited

First published in Great Britain 1994

© David M. Martin 1994

British Library Cataloguing in Publication Data
A CIP catalogue record for this book can be obtained
from the British Library

ISBN 0 273 60729 4

All rights reserved; no part of this publication may be
reproduced, stored in a retrieval system, or transmitted in
any form or by any means, electronic, mechanical, photocopying,
recording, or otherwise without either the prior written permission
of the Publishers or a licence permitting restricted copying
in the United Kingdom issued by the Copyright Licensing Agency Ltd,
90 Tottenham Court Road, London W1P 9HE. This book may not be lent,
resold, hired out or otherwise disposed of by way of trade in any form
of binding or cover other than that in which it is published, without
the prior consent of the Publishers.

1 3 5 7 9 10 8 6 4 2

Photoset in Century Schoolbook by
Northern Phototypesetting Co. Ltd, Bolton

Printed and bound by Antony Rowe Ltd, Eastbourne

*The Publishers' policy is to use paper manufactured
from sustainable forests.*

Contents

■

Introduction

∎

Ideally we would satisfy all of our customers all of the time. Realistically most organisations know that this is virtually impossible. It is almost inevitable that we shall have to deal with some dissatisfied customers at some time. There is little that is difficult about dealing with customer complainants, though dealing with difficult customers may be demanding. Sadly it seems that because many organisations fail to do the former effectively, they end up having to do the latter. Further, in failing to deal adequately with customers at an initial stage, they actually may create their own demanding customers who are, by definition, far more difficult to deal with. It must be better to avoid the difficult encounter with the demanding customer, rather than needing to deal with it. This is possible by greater attention to the basics – terms, training, and temperament. If these aspects of our businesses are not addressed, then the problems of demanding customers will plague us, wasting our time, resources and efforts in the process. Further, as research demonstrates, failure to deal effectively with complainants can cost our organisations dearly. Sixty per cent of dissatisfied complainants will not repurchase from their supplier, whilst one leading UK company states that a person with a bad experience is likely to inform up to 17 other potential customers – 'hell hath no fury like a dissatisfied complainant'. Conversely, where complaints are dealt with satisfactorily 80 per cent will repurchase and will also spread the good news, acting as unpaid promotion agents.

This book uses real-life case studies to illustrate the practical suggestions and recommendations included. The examples demonstrate bad practices as well as good, on the premise that it is sometimes easier to learn from our mistakes than our successes. The case studies illustrate practices and also draw conclusions why particular approaches did or did not work. Whilst urging consideration of these practical approaches, the examples and the lessons and inferences drawn therefrom should only ever be used as guides. All instances are different, and even though it may appear superficially similar, an approach that worked in a particular case must not be regarded as an absolute criterion. 'Circumstances do alter cases' and this is never more true than in attempting to deal with customers and their problems. Often of course there can be more than one possible solution, and in training those we require to deal with customers we need to:

- adopt parameters that illustrate the manner in which we wish to do business, without restricting flexibility or innovation
- provide guidelines under which we can 'do a deal' rather than hard and fast rules, and
- allow discretion to manoeuvre rather than impose narrow limits of action which may otherwise hamper common sense reactions.

The conclusions which are drawn from the case studies and recommendations put forward are intended not as a complete answer to a problem – indeed there is often no complete 'right' answer. The aim is to provide suggestions, examples and illustrations – not as a panacea to solve all difficult customer encounters but as a prompt for further thought within the reader's specific area of operation.

Sadly, good quality customer care and service tends to be the exception rather than the rule in the UK. If we do not provide this, then, in the competitive nineties and the first years of the new millennium, it may be impossible to escape the almost inevitable reaction of such attitudes – our customers voting for our competitors with their feet and their wallets. The avoidance of this damaging scenario is entirely possible but requires thought, preparation and commitment at all levels.

Dealing with demanding customers is my third book for this Institute of Management series. *Tough talking* considered the nature of the desired result we wish to achieve from every encounter and the ways and means by which we can help ensure that we can always achieve those results. *Manipulating meetings* examined ways in which we could ensure that we successfully achieve our aims when subjects are discussed within the context of a meeting, and ways in which we could help ensure our meetings are productive. In both titles, real-life case studies were used as here to illustrate theory and practice. Whilst most of the case studies featured in this title are entirely new, I have re-used a few featured in those earlier books and also a few from my earlier book *How to control your costs and increase your profits* (Directors Books, 1992) where these seemed particularly appropriate. The common thread is the achievement of our ultimate aim – whether it is

Introduction

∎

Ideally we would satisfy all of our customers all of the time. Realistically most organisations know that this is virtually impossible. It is almost inevitable that we shall have to deal with some dissatisfied customers at some time. There is little that is difficult about dealing with customer complainants, though dealing with difficult customers may be demanding. Sadly it seems that because many organisations fail to do the former effectively, they end up having to do the latter. Further, in failing to deal adequately with customers at an initial stage, they actually may create their own demanding customers who are, by definition, far more difficult to deal with. It must be better to avoid the difficult encounter with the demanding customer, rather than needing to deal with it. This is possible by greater attention to the basics – terms, training, and temperament. If these aspects of our businesses are not addressed, then the problems of demanding customers will plague us, wasting our time, resources and efforts in the process. Further, as research demonstrates, failure to deal effectively with complainants can cost our organisations dearly. Sixty per cent of dissatisfied complainants will not repurchase from their supplier, whilst one leading UK company states that a person with a bad experience is likely to inform up to 17 other potential customers – 'hell hath no fury like a dissatisfied complainant'. Conversely, where complaints are dealt with satisfactorily 80 per cent will repurchase and will also spread the good news, acting as unpaid promotion agents.

This book uses real-life case studies to illustrate the practical suggestions and recommendations included. The examples demonstrate bad practices as well as good, on the premise that it is sometimes easier to learn from our mistakes than our successes. The case studies illustrate practices and also draw conclusions why particular approaches did or did not work. Whilst urging consideration of these practical approaches, the examples and the lessons and inferences drawn therefrom should only ever be used as guides. All instances are different, and even though it may appear superficially similar, an approach that worked in a particular case must not be regarded as an absolute criterion. 'Circumstances do alter cases' and this is never more true than in attempting to deal with customers and their problems. Often of course there can be more than one possible solution, and in training those we require to deal with customers we need to:

– adopt parameters that illustrate the manner in which we wish to do business, without restricting flexibility or innovation
– provide guidelines under which we can 'do a deal' rather than hard and fast rules, and
– allow discretion to manoeuvre rather than impose narrow limits of action which may otherwise hamper common sense reactions.

The conclusions which are drawn from the case studies and recommendations put forward are intended not as a complete answer to a problem – indeed there is often no complete 'right' answer. The aim is to provide suggestions, examples and illustrations – not as a panacea to solve all difficult customer encounters but as a prompt for further thought within the reader's specific area of operation.

Sadly, good quality customer care and service tends to be the exception rather than the rule in the UK. If we do not provide this, then, in the competitive nineties and the first years of the new millennium, it may be impossible to escape the almost inevitable reaction of such attitudes – our customers voting for our competitors with their feet and their wallets. The avoidance of this damaging scenario is entirely possible but requires thought, preparation and commitment at all levels.

Dealing with demanding customers is my third book for this Institute of Management series. *Tough talking* considered the nature of the desired result we wish to achieve from every encounter and the ways and means by which we can help ensure that we can always achieve those results. *Manipulating meetings* examined ways in which we could ensure that we successfully achieve our aims when subjects are discussed within the context of a meeting, and ways in which we could help ensure our meetings are productive. In both titles, real-life case studies were used as here to illustrate theory and practice. Whilst most of the case studies featured in this title are entirely new, I have re-used a few featured in those earlier books and also a few from my earlier book *How to control your costs and increase your profits* (Directors Books, 1992) where these seemed particularly appropriate. The common thread is the achievement of our ultimate aim – whether it is in negotiation, in meetings or in dealing with customers. All too often it is simply the fact that we lose sight of (or fail to establish) that ultimate aim that leads us into problems that could have been avoided with a little thought, preparation and consideration. Nowhere is this more true than in dealing with demanding customers.

David M. Martin

May 1994

1

Scene setting

Key learning points

1 In dealing with demanding customers we need to identify the problem, to avoid the incidence and to recognise our end aim.

2 Differing standards can cause demanding customers and difficult encounters.

3 Consumer demand is changing rapidly – we must respond to changes.

4 We must retain existing, as well as acquire new customers.

There is little about dealing with demanding customers that is any different from dealing with any other management problem, except that, since we are dealing with people the challenges may be somewhat more varied. As with other management problems we need to:

- Identify the challenge
- Avoid the incidence of the encounters that must otherwise must be resolved
- Recognise and always remember our ultimate aim without overlooking the fact that such aim(s) may differ from that of the person(s) with whom we will be interfacing
- Realise that we and our customer may have different standards which need to be reconciled, and not least
- Consider the changing face of consumer demands and expectations.

Identify the challenge

In an ideal world all our products and services would always be up to the specification required, delivered on time, and be to the complete satisfaction of our customers. Sadly, such Utopian ideals probably only existed in the imagination and writings of Sir Thomas More four hundred years ago. Although, overall standards of work and performance have no doubt improved since then, and the advent of machinery has aided the maintenance of standard quality, we are still a long way from this ideal. Indeed, despite absolute adherence to the principles and practice of BS5750, the quality standard, as well as the origination of precise specifications for every endeavour, and training and coaching all our employees, it would still be unrealistic to expect that we can completely eliminate mistakes and errors, missed deadlines, poor quality, and so on. In short the errors that lead to customer complaints will continue and the best we can do is to reduce them to a bare minimum. Realising the essential truth of this contention of course begs the question 'what do we do about it?' Since we know we cannot always achieve perfection, there will be occasions when we need to interface with a customer whose impression of our goods and services does not accord with the standards we wish to provide. The reality of the situation is that there will be problem encounters caused by our falling short of our standards. We need to plan for these encounters and endeavour to 'train out' the incidence.

Case study 1.1
Nice return

A report in January 1994 in Personnel Management highlighted a £7 million training exercise undertaken by British Telecom. BT line managers were asked to estimate the cost of errors committed by junior managers in a year. The figure of £200 million was arrived at and included costs related to missing deadlines, poor diagnosis of problems, inefficient budgeting AND ... not dealing with customer complaints. After training, the improvement in performance was measured and it was calculated that the improvement was worth all the missing £200 million plus a further £70 million – a figure verified by the company accountants.

It may cause unease to realise that our organisations cannot always attain the required standards, but at least if we set such standards we have a criteria. If such standards are lacking then we have no hope of attaining them, no hope of satisfying most of our customers most of the time and we are simply running up costs – as the BT survey showed.

Case study 1.2
At least that's what we want

British Gas, like BT also recently privatised, issued a statement of purpose in 1992. It reads (extract only) 'We aim to be a world class energy company and the leading international gas business, by ... satisfying our customers' wishes for excellent quality of service and outstanding value ... '. Having thus stated this aim (amongst others) to its' customers, the company has publicly affirmed its commitment to the quality ethic.

> **Key technique**
> This provides a criterion for those at the sharp end, that is those who actually interface with the customer, often in the latter's home.

Case study 1.3
This is our commitment

Similarly, Eastern Electricity, another privatised company, issued a list of guarantees to their customers starting with the introduction 'Concern for our customers has always been one of the hallmarks of Eastern Electricity. To make certain our service to you is always as good as possible, we have developed a Guaranteed Customer Service scheme ... '.

> **Key technique**
> Here is another example of a company publicly nailing its colours to the mast and advertising what it is doing so that all involved are aware.

Realistically companies like BT, British Gas and Eastern Electricity are unlikely to be able to please all their customers all the time but at least they have set out their standards for all to see. The criteria are there and their presence alone exerts pressure on those at the sharp end to ensure compliance.

Avoid the incidence

Like the advice given to the would-be litigant 'the best way to win at law is to avoid it, since even if you win you will probably lose', the best advice in considering how to deal with demanding customers must be to try to avoid the necessity of having to deal with as many of them as possible in the first place – one of the main themes adopted in this book. In other words we should strive to 'design out' the source of the conflict to avoid the possibility of the war starting, rather than simply preparing for battle. After all, if we could avoid the incidents that create demanding customers then we would have no need to consider the ways and means of dealing with them. We would also save our organisations a vast amount of time, effort and resources, as well as avoiding damaging a reputation that may have taken years to build.

Case study 1.4
Queue definitely not jumping

In a local main post office the queue had reached the door and despite there being spaces for 8 assistants to serve, only two were open for business. It took 16 minutes for the customer to reach a counter, by which time her normal placid temperament was somewhat strained. 'I've come to collect our order of stamps' she said to the clerk. The order could not be found. 'Do you mean that having 'phoned me to say it was ready and having waited a quarter of an hour to be served, you can't find it and I've got to go through the whole farrago again – you're utterly incompetent'.

Key technique
If to suit the post office's convenience it was easier to leave an order to await collection, the least that should have been done was to have a nominated place for such collections.

Remedial action
Whilst the British are said to be the best nationality for queuing in the world, expecting customers to queue for this length of time is both insulting to those who ultimately pay the wages of the organisation and needlessly aggravating, creating demanding customers where none previously existed.

Being currently a state owned monopoly protects such organisations from real market demand and customer requirements. Those organisations without the benefit of a monopoly, however, do have to take note and react to customer demands. Failing to satisfy customers is inherently expensive – as BT found.

4

Case study 1.5
Costing the complaint

A company in the leisure industry was concerned at the falling amount of its repeat business, which it rightly regarded as the cornerstone of its continued success, and conducted a survey which showed, amongst other results, that customers were being lost through a failure to deal with initial, sometimes quite minor, concerns. Because these concerns were not being given the attention the customers felt they deserved one of two alternatives then occurred. Either the customer voted with their feet and went to a competitor (which meant the company then had to invest heavily to replace their lost custom – see Chapter 2) or senior management were involved as the customer took the matter further. An external consultant investigated the problem and, as well as identifying a number of improvements, pointed out that the cost in management time spent investigating the problems, the loss of resources in telephone calls, correspondence and refund of expenses to complainants was in excess of £100 per complaint, ignoring the cost of any refund or restitution related to the actual product and service.

Key technique
The fact that such costs are hidden does not mean they do not damage the organisation. Time spent placating customers is not being spent driving the organisation forward.

Remedial action
The introduction of a complaint cost analysis form (see Chapter 6) can concentrate the mind on the problem and lead to improvements.

Recognise the ultimate aim

In every problem encounter there will be two viewpoints – that of the customer who is dissatisfied with some aspect of the performance of the supplier and that of the supplier who needs to respond to that dissatisfaction. In dealing with such an encounter the supplier is placed in the position of negotiator and as such needs both to take and to retain the initiative. This is essential in order to ensure that there is continual movement towards a result. Of course, it may be that there is more than one method of reaching the desired result and the negotiator needs to retain a flexible approach to the means by which the aim is attained. The recognition and constant awareness of one's own and one's opponent's desired result is essential in seeking to resolve demanding situations. This entails treating each case on its merits and being open minded about possible solutions, striving to convert the customer's attitude from one of complaint to one of satisfaction in order to protect the reputation of the supplier and engender a continuation of their custom.

For example:

■ If there is a problem with a disruptive employee, the desired result must be the ending of such disruption so that everyone can resume normal working. That result can be achieved either by the conversion of the disruptive employee to the required way of working or by his/her removal.

■ If the problem concerns a dispute over the terms of trade with another supplier, the desired result is the resumption of supplies to the organisation on acceptable terms. This can be achieved by sourcing supplies elsewhere (with all the potential inherent downside that such new relationships may entail), or reaching a mutually acceptable compromise or agreement with the existing supplier.

■ If there is a justifiable complaint by a customer, the desired result should be rectifying any loss to the customer, whilst protecting the good name of the organisation. A reputation that has taken years to build can be lost in a matter of minutes. (See case study 12.1.)

■ If there is an unjustifiable complaint, it is necessary to recognise that what may seem unjustifiable to the supplier may be wholly justifiable to the customer. The compliant can be dealt with by refusing to countenance it, or by seeking to convert the complaint to satisfaction if a suitable compromise can be reached without major cost, or the creation of a potentially dangerous precedent. The supplier needs to bear in mind the potential downside in terms of adverse publicity.

Each of these examples entails a degree of negotiation, rather than a refusal to countenance any view other than one's own.

Negotiation is not weakness, it is a pragmatic approach towards the reconciliation of differing views, both of which may be valid, and for this reason, even though the desired result must be kept firmly as the negotiator's priority, it may be necessary to dilute one or both parties' expectations, i.e. to move towards a compromise.

Recognition of different standards or expectations

'Hype' is short for hyperbole meaning a statement which exaggerates and is not meant to be taken literally. In marketing our products and services, hype tends to be used to a greater or lesser degree. However, we need to take care that we do not 'over hype', expectations of worth or quality, thus creating higher expectations than we can deliver. If our organisation does indulge in this then we can expect a greater number of demanding customers and greater difficulties in trying to satisfy them. There are always two sides to every problem and to be successful in dealing with the demanding, we need always to determine the reality of the other party's viewpoint bearing in mind the expectations that we have created in the mind of the customer. The problem of differing standards can be even more basic than that created by advertising or promotional material. It can be reduced to a basic understanding of, and commitment to, manners, a comprehension of the other person's rights in the widest sense of the word. It is not only courteous to hold doors open for those about to use the doorway, or to offer a seat to an elderly or incapacitated traveller, it is an indication of standards. The act is beneficial to both donor and recipient and in a world full of pressure and stress, can make both 'feel good'. Writing on this subject in the *Mail on Sunday* in December 1993, the Duke of Devonshire related a tale of a taxi driver to whom he had simply said 'Thank you very much, that's very kind'. The taxi driver replied 'You don't know what a difference it makes you saying that'. The Duke went on 'manners are like a friendly disease, perhaps if you pass them on, more and more people become infected'. 'Infected' or not, we are less likely to be difficult customers if we 'feel good' than if we have been poorly treated, like the customer in case study 1.4.

The changing face of consumer demand – and demanding consumers

'Demand' is used here in the context of the expectation the customer has as a result of his money being exchanged for goods or services provided. This is an ongoing requirement as customers' viewpoints are continually changing. This in turn will have a considerable impact on the way in which we handle and attempt to resolve such encounters. In the mid 1980s the United Kingdom enjoyed a period of 'super confidence'. It seemed the decline of the country from its former status as a world power and the demise of its Empire had been arrested, that British made goods and services were once more in worldwide and constant demand, and that wealth creation by and for the majority was virtually guaranteed. Many people were able to make a great deal of money by exploiting opportunities and cashing in on the rapid increase in consumer spending power which led to a nationwide boom. Unfortunately the apparent promise of a long term high demand economy of those years proved to be illusory and within a very short time the country was in recession, consumer confidence had reached an all-time low and demand had slumped. The slow rate of recovery under-lined the damage done to the manufacturing base of what was once the greatest trading nation in the world. Important though this was, of far greater import in terms of demand recovery was the severe damage that the recession had done to long term consumer confidence. Fear of losing employment became an overwhelming constraint on those whose purchasing power was otherwise undiminished. Thus even when the recession eased and confidence began to return, consumer demand and spending only did so extremely slowly and cautiously. Indeed, at one time savings as a percentage of earnings doubled indicating that consumers were far more prepared to save than to spend.

Losing the spending habit

In turn this led to two phenomena – firstly UK consumers had got out of the habit of discretionary spending, and, secondly, they became far more discerning than had previously been the case. The 'throw away' society of the 80s was transformed into the 'make it last' society of the 90s.

Case study 1.6
Creatures of habit

The shop was extremely profitable mainly because at meal break times in the large factory opposite, its otherwise low customer flow was swollen by well over 100 customers requiring snacks and confectionery. However, one year the employees who worked at the factory went on strike for several weeks. The shop manager who had seen his trade and profit severely dented, eagerly awaited the resumption of normal trade on the first day after the settlement of the strike. Although some of the old customers came as usual, many did not. When he investigated he found that some now brought sandwiches, whilst others bought their snacks on the way to work and had no need to visit his shop during the break and still others had got badly into debt during the strike and were restricting their expenditure to pay off such debts. Slowly trade did increase but a year later it had still not recovered to anywhere near its pre-strike level.

Key technique
Customers are creatures of habit – break the habit and the effects can be far-reaching. Break the confidence of regular income and every item of expenditure is closely examined for value.

Remedial action: Promotion (possibly with discount voucher) to remind people of the facility and to tempt them back to the outlet, plus excellent service.

9

Expenditure attitudes

Obviously many of the companies that were best able to survive the recession were those who examined budgets and expenditure carefully; equally the consumers best placed to survive were those who had not lived to the limit (or beyond) of their expenditure. Many of those not covered by these descriptions suffered badly or did not survive. The survivors, either because of their original conservative attitudes or because they recognised the painful lessons of the recession, found their attitudes to consumption hardening. In short, many corporate and private consumers very swiftly became far more discerning and demanding in terms of quality and value, than hitherto had been the case.

Case study 1.7
'Make what you can sell – don't sell what you can make'

Until 1979 the Maynards Group could sell as much sugar confectionery as its two factories could make. Indeed, the sales and profitability of the Group's confectionery manufacturing division were constrained not by the market but by the factory output capacity. The UK budget of 1979, which virtually doubled VAT from a rate of 8 per cent to 15 per cent, changed that situation at a stroke. Sugar confectionery with 15 per cent VAT imposed could no longer compete easily with some of the food products (which bore no VAT) for which it was often a substitute. In the following four years, another period of UK recession, the UK sugar confectionery market shrank by virtually 25 per cent. It took considerable ingenuity to compensate for this loss of demand caused entirely by a pricing policy over which the company had no control. During those four years the company outperformed the market by introducing new products, better marketing and packaging and more aggressive selling. Some of these changes posed difficulties, but the greatest difficulty was to get the management to accept the sea-change of approach to making what it could sell – basic preconceptions and attitudes had to be altered to cope with market conditions which totally changed.

10

Remedial action
Constant re-assessment of what the market really wants must be

Growing consumer power

These changes of habit and of basics epitomise the challenge for UK companies interfacing with their customers in the 1990s. Over-buoyant demand is, other than in a few fortunate sectors, a thing of the past and we must deal with a new situation. That situation is one where the customer is king. If low demand is endemic, then we must take care of, indeed even court, those customers who remain. This seems obvious and yet, as is demonstrated in some of the case studies included here, more than a few organisations do not yet seem to have realised such a basic truth.

Case study 1.8
Miserly with the goods as well

In the eastern part of England the recession coincided with an official drought which lasted (as far as consumers being unable to use their hoses) for over two years. In the middle of the drought there was national press advertising for a device called a rain miser which enabled householders to capture rain water *via* a siphoning device within the domestic downpipes. In reply to sending an order for one a customer received the following missive '*Thank you for your recent order. We are out of stock and have therefore had to cancel your order*'. They should be so lucky to be in such a position at such a time!

Remedial action

If there were no alternative products that could have been offered, and no possibility of the company re-ordering the goods and being re-supplied, the suggestion of an alternative supplier for the original product would at least repair some of damage otherwise done to the supplier's reputation.

The discerning older customer

The UK has a rapidly ageing population. As consumers age, many tend to find themselves with increased purchasing power, since over the years they will have accumulated most of the things that they rate as being essential to maintain them in the lifestyle to which they have become accustomed, whilst simultaneously many of their financial commitments disappear. In addition the current 'parent generation' is, despite the recession, likely to be one of increasing purchasing power, not least because of the considerable amount of wealth it will inherit from its own property-owning parents. It is estimated that by the year 2000, demand for shares on the Stock Exchange will have increased by around 5 per cent due to a desire, or even need, to invest some of such inherited funds. This sector of the market is thus likely to have funds available, yet, having been through some austere periods, may tend to be far more discerning and reticent about spending than its offspring. In addition, these consumers may be far more demanding in terms of range, quality and value for money, and more prepared to voice such demands. Since experience increases with age, they will also be well-versed in ensuring that, should goods and services not attain the standards they desire, pressure is exerted to rectify this. Unlike many of the younger generation they will have experienced a time when second best would not 'do' and when mistakes were far rarer and far less condoned than apparently is the case now.

11

Case study 1.9
One way out

The elderly customer had been waiting to be served in the local unit of a national retail chain. Whilst the shop appeared busy, he had observed some of the young assistants chatting rather than actually serving. He approached two of them.

'Excuse me, I've been waiting five minutes for someone to give me some information about these electrical appliances.'

'We're very busy.'

'The shop certainly is, and there are several customers waiting to be served, but you two seem to be chatting.'

'No ,we're very busy.'

'Well in that case, there's an easy answer – you can have these back' (dumping the items in their hands) *'and I'll walk out – that's one customer fewer isn't it – and if you lose a few more customers, the shop won't be able to afford to pay you to chat to one another.'*

12

Key technique

Needless to say, the chain's managing director was not best pleased when the customer wrote to him to highlight the incident. In the competitive world in which we now trade, there is usually some other trader who will be only too delighted to serve the customers we disappoint.

The European perspective

Membership of the European Community led to UK participation in the market 'sans frontiéres'. Although ready, many of those UK companies that had prepared for additional European demand for their goods from New Year's Day 1993, found little in evidence, mainly since European consumers were suffering from the same malady that had affected the UK's home markets for the previous two years. In fact in many of the other European countries it seems that the repercussions of their recessions may be felt for much longer than may be the case in the UK.

Still considering the European dimension a similar ageing population syndrome exists there with problems and opportunities similar to those already noted in the UK, save that our European neighbours tend to be far less reticent about complaining if products and services do not live up to their high standards.

Case study 1.10
No slip up

The German car manufacturer was being shown round a newly refurbished vehicle production works in the north of England. The floor had been treated with a special compound which virtually eliminated dust. The Production Manager proudly explained the advantages of the surface, but admitted that since engine oil could reduce its sealing powers they had to use drip trays under the vehicles. 'We too use a floor sealant like this' commented the German engineer, 'but we do not need drip trays'. 'Is your floor surface resistant to oil then?' enquired the UK manager. 'It does not need to be – German engines do not leak oil', was the quiet and confident reply.

Remedial action
Emulate competitors' standards or lose custom.

It's a hard competitive world, and it takes no hostages. But if we are in, and want to stay in, then in order to ensure we satisfy our customers we must be able to compete with the best, both in terms of quality of product and in quality of service – before, during and after sale. This will, quite rightly, be regarded by many as stating the obvious and yet, as some of the case studies in this book demonstrate, very often in the UK corporate self-satisfaction is more widely perceived than customer-satisfaction. This attitude was highlighted by President of the Board of Trade, Michael Heseltine, in an address in November 1993, when he accused British management in general of being complacent about quality, performance and output.

A dynamic perspective

With difficult trade terms, rising costs and enhanced consumer requirements, the one essential is to hold on to our existing customer base, and when there are customer problems, to deal with them in a positive and practical way that will not just deal with the problem and rectify the situation, but also seek to convert the demanding customer into a satisfied one, and ideally a repeat one. If demand is slack it is essential that we retain our customers – it is far more cost-effective to retain an existing customer than to source a new one.

13

Money talks – so must we

Key learning points

1 Retaining existing customers is not only easier than sourcing new ones, it also costs a lot less.

2 Positive action to retain customers, including those who complain is necessary.

3 Complaints are caused – often by our own fault. We must accept responsibility for rectification which includes restoring customer choice.

4 Providing channels for customer complaints can help defuse complaints.

With tight demand and competitive trade, retaining existing customers must be a priority. After all those who already buy from us have a knowledge of our products and services and confidence that what they are buying is worth their investment. The longer we can retain customers the greater the time and number of purchases over which can be spread the 'cost' of acquiring them. If we retain all our customers we need spend nothing to attract new customers to maintain the *status quo*. Conversely if we lose 10 per cent of our customers each year then over a 10 year period the whole customer base will have been lost unless we invest in attracting new customers. Replacing 10 per cent each year may not be too difficult a task but if our customers are dissatisfied with our performance or with our service, or with the way in which their demands are considered and treated, these replacement costs can rise steeply. In a survey of the top 200 UK companies, consultants Price Waterhouse found that barely 10 per cent analyse how many customers they lose each year, and yet the firm estimated that customer defection loses British industry around £100 billion each year, whilst a similar amount is spent on marketing, sales and distribution expenses. Retaining satisfied customers requires an investment in customer commitment and care far less costly than customer replacement. However, losing those that you have acquired by such investment, merely as a result of poor customer attention is the most costly process of all.

Case study 2.1
Care-less

The family had been going to the hotel regularly. On their last visit, however, they were given a very sub-standard room and it was obvious that the high standards of service and food provided by the previous owners had been discarded by the new owners. Prices had increased whereas standards of service had plummeted and the attitude of most of the new, short-service staff that had replaced the former long service staff was off-hand and casual. In discussing this with other guests it became clear that they had similar opinions and did not intend returning.

In complaining of this deterioration of the value being given, the former guest pointed out that many of the failings were not cost- but standard-related, and, since the hotel had numerous competitors, there was an urgent need for a re-think to avoid a complete loss of business.

15

> **Key technique**
> Establishing 'a requirement for success' criterion is essential. Here, that criterion was the retention of repeat custom to achieve basic room occupancy. Attraction of new and additional guests was also important but the retention of former guests was critical. In failing to concentrate on the basics, the management had created a situation that encouraged complaint – costly to deal with and dangerous to their ongoing reputation. In addition, dealing with 'complaints and repairs' is a dilution of managerial attention.

Customer retention

Writing in the Harvard Business Review in early 1993, Frederick Reichheld, Director of Consultancy at Bain & Company, underlined the need exemplified in case study 2.1, with the comment 'customer loyalty appears to be the only way to achieve sustainably superior profits'. He used as an example the life assurance business stating that a 5 per cent increase in customer retention has the effect of lowering costs per policy by 18 per cent – no small cost in any business. Similarly, MBNA, an American credit card company, found that a 5 per cent rise in customer loyalty led to a 60 per cent increase in profits after five years.

Case study 2.2
Who cares?

The customer, being very much a person of habit, always visited a national chain store whenever she went shopping. On one visit she wished to buy some items on display and asked an assistant to obtain them from the store room. Having waited patiently for at least five minutes, the assistant returned, but before reaching the customer, was stopped by another assistant who wanted advice regarding another enquiry. When she had finished, the assistant returned to the customer with the news that the item was not in stock. Somewhat irritated by both the wait and the interruption, the customer selected an alternative item and asked for that. The assistant again went to the stock room, again there was a wait, again she was interrupted before she got back to the customer and again the item was not in stock.

'I really don't know why you have all these items on display when you don't have them in stock.'

The assistant shrugged *'Nothing to do with me.'*

'Neither, I suppose, is the fact that I have now been waiting for over ten minutes, some of which time was wasted by your dealing with other assistants' questions – and at no time have you offered an apology. I am disgusted with this and intend taking my custom elsewhere.'

16

Remedial action

Whilst being out of stock was not the responsibility of the assistant, ensuring that the customer was treated with courtesy (by apologising for the situation and the delay) that, as the first call on her time, other assistant's questions were deferred until the customer had been attended to, were priorities. Similarly, retaining the customer's goodwill despite the situation was a further priority completely overlooked. Far from retaining the customer, the encounter needlessly generated a degree of extra aggravation. The customer might have been aggravated by finding items on display were not in stock when there was no warning that this might be the case, but the delays should, and could, have been avoided.

The incident related in case study 2.2 took place in the buoyant years of the late 1980s. Within three years that chain, in common with a number of other UK chains, had introduced a points based discount card, the sole basis of which was to address the need to boost customer retention and provide a reward for customer loyalty. A report published in late 1993 on research by the Cranfield School of Management indicated that loyal customers spend up to four times more in their first-choice stores than those who have developed no such loyalty. Whilst the discount cards do promote loyalty, it is at the expense of a diminution of profit margin.

After all, if a store earns 10 per cent profit on sales and gives a 10 per cent discount to buy loyalty, it must generate an additional 11 per cent of sales just to 'mark time' and fund the 'lost' discounted sales. As far as the store cited in case study 2.2 is concerned, better customer care at the sharp end would have been far less costly.

The customer is treasurer

Some organisations fail to realise the most essential rule of business – **the customer pays for everything**. This rule is fundamental, applies to all organisations, irrespective of size or trade, and yet is often overlooked. Everything our businesses buy (including our own wages and salaries) can be paid for only if the customer buys, and continues to buy, the product or service we provide. By extrapolation, only if the customer is satisfied with that product or service can there be any guarantee of a continuation of their custom and thus of the business itself. Further, only if more customers can be similarly satisfied can there be any expansion of the business. 'Keeping the customer satisfied' is going to be infinitely harder to achieve in the 1990s and the first years of the new century when many markets may not be expanding and some may, like the sugar confectionery market of the early 1980s featured in case study 1.7, be contracting. We are now trading in a very competitive age when most products and services are substitutional, when our competitors will be seeking to take away our customers and our business, and when consumer choice is likely to be at its most powerful. Only the best will survive and if we wish to be among the survivors we need to ensure our organisations are among the best. Obviously this entails our product or service being sound, in demand and of good value and of all of this being correctly perceived by our target audience of customers. Perhaps less obviously it entails a need to deal with customers positively, respecting their rights and power. Unless we treat them correctly we may find ourselves unable to treat them at all.

The recipe for today

When trade is slack, every sale achieves a great significance particularly if it was achieved at the expense of profit margin. Whilst this should be self-evident, it cannot be taken for granted that everyone in the organisation appreciates it, and we need to train and develop the workforce to understand these realities of economic life. Failing the customer may not only lose a sale and the possibility of a repeat order, but will also incur additional costs. Whether these are costs borne in terms of restitution, a cost in terms of the time involved or a cost in terms of lost repeat sales, dissatisfied customers can cost our organisations dearly.

If we can keep our customer, and more of them, satisfied, we can reduce costs and save money. It is not just that the money is saved of course, as the real value is that every £1 of saving from costs flows through to additional profit.

18

---

a) If company A is making 10 per cent profit on its sales then every £1 saved from its expenditure means it needs to generate £10 less sales to achieve the same profit:
- ii)   Sales £100 less costs £90 = £10 profit
- iii) Sales £100 less costs £89 = £11 profit or
- iiii) Sales £110 less costs £99 = £11 profit

With the level of profit return on sales in i), to increase profits the choice needs to be made between increasing sales by 10 per cent as in iii) (which might have the effect of increasing costs in proportion – a factor which is ignored here) or reducing costs by £1 as in ii). Sales, particularly in a recession, may be hard to come by and in any event are not under our control whereas our costs are. Thus by saving £1 on our costs we can, if we wish, avoid the need to find £10 of sales, and our sales target is unchanged.

b) There is a further dimension to this since if we can shave 10 per cent off our costs **and** maintain our sales we can virtually double our profit:
- i)   Sales £100 less costs £90 = £10 profit
- ii) Sales £100 less costs (£90 – 10%) £81 = £19

c) We can really make things happen if we can shave our costs by 10 per cent **and** increase our sales by 10 per cent:
- i)   Sales £100 less costs £90 = £10 profit
- ii) Sales (up 10%) £110 less costs (minus 10%) £81 = £29 profit

---

Fig. 2.1 Using cost-reduction as a profit multiplier
(from the author's 'How to control your costs and increase your profits')

Getting the financial facts across

Comprehension of the financial impact of poor customer service can be difficult, particularly for younger personnel, since they may find it difficult to link their work to the customer.

Regardless of this difficulty of comprehension this link and all it entails it is essential, as very often it is those self-same younger personnel who are placed at the cutting edge – actually dealing with customers. Their performing well is essential to the reputation and existence of the business. Whilst this was always the case, given the current and anticipated changes to consumer demand and rights, the need to train everyone to provide the appropriate responses and to court the customer, particularly if a mistake has been made, is paramount. It is widely accepted that a high employee turnover can be a major cause of customer dissatisfaction. Not only will the organisation be losing employees with a better product knowledge but long-serving employees tend to be more *au fait* with what loyal customers want, as was the case in the hotel in case study 2.1.

Case study 2.3
Poor vision

The print on packaging becoming ever smaller, I needed spectacles but dislike carrying expensive glasses when out shopping. An advertisement for folding glasses seemed to solve the problem and I telephoned an order, paying by credit card. Nothing was heard for eight weeks although I noted that the amount had been debited from my credit card.

On telephoning the company, the bored voice of a young girl mumbled the question 'Was the magnification three dioptres?' I confirmed this was so, and was then told that in that case they were still awaiting delivery which was expected 'very soon'. I enquired why in that case they had debited my account six weeks previously. 'That's for security – we can't leave cheques lying around here.' 'But this is an Access debit.' Silence. Since at this point not a single word of apology for the delay had been offered I cancelled the order. Even in doing that, 'bored voice' had to be reminded that as well as my name and address they would want the Access account details in order to refund the amount taken.

> **Result**
> One lost order, one set of costs with no revenue, one dissatisfied customer and one potentially adverse public relations sore.

Remedial action

1. Ensure all telesales personnel are monitored for helpfulness and customer care.
2. Always apologise (even where unnecessary) as it aids rapport.
3. Be alert and understand the customer's viewpoint.

In fact, this company redeemed itself by means of a personally telephoned apology from the Managing Director who undertook to ensure that such a poor advertisement for his company was not repeated. 'Bored voice' should not be blamed out of hand as obviously she may not have had the benefit of a proper training programme, or, if she had, her performance was not being monitored. Having said that, however, one would have thought that simple basic courtesy could have overcome this problem encounter.

An alternative scenario

'*Bloggs Mail Order company – Jackie speaking – can I help you?*'

'*I placed an order on 24th August but have heard nothing and find you have already debited my Access account with the cost.*'

'*Could I have your name sir and the product you ordered?*'

'*Mr Martin and the order was for a pair of triple-magnification folding spectacles.*'

'*Oh I am so sorry Mr Martin, we had such a demand as a result of that advertisement that we used all our ready stock and our reserve stock and are waiting for the replacement stock which should be in any day now.*'

'*Well why have you debited my Access account?*'

'*That's for security reasons – usually we aim to despatch the goods within seven days of making the debit but this time we got caught out by the demand – I am so sorry you have been kept waiting but we should be able to despatch the glasses within the next seven days, or else we can credit your Access account today – whichever you would prefer.*'

Key techniques

(1) Using her own name as well as that of the customer creates a rapport between assistant and customer.

(2) A crisp business-like response provides an impression of efficiency.

(3) The obvious knowledge of the reason for the problem also aids rapport with the customer. Nothing irritates customers more than to raise a problem and find that the other person knows nothing of it, and it is impossible to be put through to someone who does. Ignorance aggravates frustration.

(4) The immediate apology should mollify all but the most demanding customers.

(5) Offering the customer the choice of money back or waiting a little longer returns control of the encounter to the customer. If this had been the instant response, in all probability the order would not have been cancelled and despite the original discourtesy, the sale would have been preserved.

Very often the problem with this type of selling is that the advertiser has no, or little, ready stock and thus if demand exceeds that anticipated, customers are kept waiting. This is a classic way of creating demanding customers, particularly if, as in case study 2.3, payment is collected swiftly. It is not only poor customer service it must be akin to fraud.

Customer control

21

In buying goods or service the consumer exercises choice – the choice to spend or not to spend. In exchanging money for goods or services the consumer judges that the goods are worth his investment. If the goods turn out to be faulty, or the service inadequate, not only is that consumer's perception of the company damaged, but also his own self-esteem, since he made the judgment to buy. In addition, and vitally important, **he has lost the essence of purchasing – his choice**. No longer does he have the capacity to buy or not to buy, or to buy an alternative product. He is locked in to the faulty product. In the suggested alternative scenario outlined in case study 2.3, Jackie restored this choice by offering alternatives back to the consumer. The proper relationship between customer and supplier was then restored and in many cases this will be sufficient to be able to deal with the demanding, and to convert a complaining customer to a satisfied one.

The challenging scenario

We therefore have a scenario in which:

■ Market demand is generally likely to lack any substantial buoyancy.

■ Products and services are increasingly substitutional.

■ Trade is becoming more competitive.

- The consumer is likely to be more discerning.

- Consumers are also becoming more aware of their rights and the advantages to be obtained from complaining if goods and services do not attain the standards they expect.

- The range and complexity of legislation with which we must comply is ever-increasing, particularly that emanating from Brussels.

All these factors have cost implications – and such costs can only be sustained, if profit margins are to be maintained, if we can pass them on to the customer. As reported in *The Observer* in late 1993, Graeme Bowler, Managing Director of Kwik Save stated that 'Quality is everything. We must get the price right before we put a wrapper on it. Everyone likes a bargain, but not one that doesn't get your shirt clean'. The kind of pressure likely to be experienced is hardly a recipe for easy success or for the faint-hearted to whom the heat of the kitchen is fatiguing rather than motivational, and is underlined by Sir John Harvey Jones's comments in *Managing to Survive*. 'I believe the 90s are going to punish those who do not think fundamentally about (their) problems.' If we need to become better at what we are doing in order to survive, interfacing with customers, and particularly interfacing when they have queries, demands or complaints is vital.

Get the basics right

Often the main problem is a lack of appreciation of the viewpoint of the customer – the person without whom the supplier cannot exist. What is evident is a lack of care for the customer's concerns, or a lack of respect for the fact that they had, in good faith, invested time and money to buy goods and services in the company concerned, only to have such confidence shattered by mistakes. In several of these case studies, the customers were not particularly demanding – they merely put forward their views with the expectation of reasonable replies, only to have their viewpoint or rights abused to the point where goodwill evaporated. In such cases the organisations actually **created** their own demanding customers.

Case study 2.4
Slow service

In 1992, on behalf of the *Sunday Times*, a correspondent wrote to 65 leading UK companies and public bodies. 'Full replies came back in anything from three to 49 days and varied from prompt, charming and informative to late, curt and rude. Nine have yet to write back despite a reminder.'

Key techniques

[1] In the article, Vincent Mitchell, lecturer in marketing at the University of Manchester, stated that the way an organisation deals with its correspondence reveals a lot about how it is run. 'How they reply is indicative of the way they view their marketplace, and an indication of the philosophy of the company.'

[2] The organisations who responded in a 'late, curt and rude' manner seem to be unaware that customer, public, and shareholder relations are a vital part of their operation and reflect how well or, in their case, how poorly they regard the customer.

[3] The enquiries were in no way demanding. Ignoring them, or answering them in a rude or curt manner is one of the best ways of ensuring that the next contact is indeed a demanding one – dealing with which could be costly.

Remedial action

Adopt as a company policy the rule that all items of correspondence will be acknowledged within 24 hours and answered, where necessary, within 15 working days.

A similar attitude to that disclosed by the *Sunday Times* article is evident in many of the case studies cited here, as often, instead of accepting complaints and dealing with them constructively the suppliers dismissed them out of hand or sought to justify an indefensible position. This negates the concept of customer respect, which is bad enough, it also courts the danger of greater protest. In exchanging cash for goods the customer expresses a confidence in the supplier. Faulty production or service shatters that confidence and removes the choice the customer formerly had. He is left with goods or services that have not lived up to the claims made for them, plus a problem and the onus for seeking a solution to that problem. Consumers can be excused for becoming annoyed when this occurs since usually they have to incur further costs to seek rectification – a principle rarely recognised, although, commendably, it was in case study 3.3. Were this situation not bad enough, if on seeking explanation or restitution the customer is then treated without respect, his views or comments given no credence and his losses ignored, it is hardly surprising if his attitude then hardens and resentment builds.

Resentment recognition

Failure to deal with a small problem courteously, effectively and efficiently at an early stage is tantamount to an invitation to turn the minor matter into a much larger problem – literally making a mountain out of a molehill. Failing to deal positively with their correspondence led several companies to find themselves named in the *Sunday Times* article. Such a reference may be shrugged off but it takes relatively little for a reputation to be lost.

In setting up systems which we can use to deal with correspondence and complaints we need to retain a perspective concerning the matter. Far better to answer and to make restitution swiftly therby negating the full effect of a complaint, even when the facts may not entirely merit it, than to resist or attempt to defend a difficult position, thereby building resentment in the other party, particularly if the cost of restitution is relatively small. After all, often the consumer is trying to deal with a problem of the supplier's, not his own, making. We need to understand that different perspective before we try to deal with it. Only if we do so will we have the correct attitude to both consumer and complaint. Failure to recognise this obligation can only create further aggravation in the long run. The longer a complaint situation is allowed to remain unresolved the more difficult it will become to resolve. The more the complainant has to attempt to put his case, the more angry and demanding he is likely to become.

Carelines

Bringing to the attention of those likely to complain the means by which they can do so may help defuse a situation. Thus many retail outlets display in their units signs setting out their way of dealing, and the Banking Ombudsman has advised banks, in view of their poor customer relations image, to display the procedure by which those who feel their treatment has been poor can lodge a complaint. Not only does this advertise to those visiting the unit the basis on which business will be conducted and their problems and concerns dealt with, but it can also act as a reminder to employees of the commitment required by the organisations.

Case study 2.5
Tanker treatment

A private motorist was furious that a tanker 'cut him up' on a main road and indeed nearly caused a serious accident as he had to brake and swerve. Part of what is regarded as justifiable anger in such circumstances is caused by the fact that usually there is little a driver can do but swallow his annoyance – indeed that is probably the safest course of action. Even if the organisation's name appears on the vehicle, there may be no easy way of contacting them, or on contacting them knowing whom to ask for to deal with the matter.

However, in this case, the motorist found that the tanker bore a notice requesting that anyone having cause to complain about the manner in which it was being driven should ring the telephone number displayed.

Key technique
The fact that he could actually report the incident to the tanker's operators played a part in reducing his anger, whilst the fact that the company openly invited calls should the behaviour offend could act as a reminder of the need to be courteous, thus avoiding the incidence of at least some demanding complaints.
At least two organisations display the name of the driver as well as a contact telephone number.

25

Many organisations now display telephone numbers on their products and encourage consumers to contact them with concerns, complaints or queries, recognising that by providing such a service an outlet for grievance and annoyance is provided which may take the sting out of many of such complaints. The provision of such 'carelines' as they are known, can also defuse problems. Thus, when rumours concerning the use of pig fat in the margarine spread 'Flora' were circulating, many concerned Jewish consumers were able to telephone the contact number on the pack to be re-assured that this was not the case.

Of course, having thus created a link with consumers, the lines can also be used to check their views on a whole range of product-related matters and indeed to its competitors. Burger-King, the fast food chain, wishing to move away from a system whereby every customer letter had to be answered by letter, encouraged customers to use a careline by displaying the contact number not only instore, but even on the customer's till receipts. In dealing with the calls the company was able to derive considerable assistance in developing its service and product range. Customers have valuable ideas about an organisation's products but few will bother to write them down. However, making a call requires less effort and is more personal.

The use of a careline tends to encourage calls of which a proportion will be hoax, or useless, or even insulting and vicious. Despite such drawbacks, the value in drawing the sting from otherwise demanding customers can be immense. It is for this reason that so many formula restaurants require waiters and waitresses to enquire whilst diners are eating their main course if everything is fine with the meal. This gives an opportunity to the diner to raise any concern, whilst if none is mentioned puts the restaurant in a strong position should complaints be voiced later. Conversely, as mentioned earlier and illustrated in case study 14.10, not having a phone number available or any means to lodge a complaint merely aggravates annoyance into anger.

3

Removing the problem source

Key learning points

1 Recognition that we cause most mistakes and thus it is our responsibility to rectify them is vital.

2 Rectifying mistakes is costly and can be even more costly in terms of lost reputation.

3 Repeat customers are the core of success for many businesses and need appropriate recognition.

4 Courtesy and forethought can negate the impact of many demanding encounters.

Before we consider further how to deal with complainants we need to understand the origin and incidence of their complaints, as our priority should be to try to reduce them as far as possible.

Mistakes do not happen – they are caused

There used to be a safety campaign which used the slogan: 'Accidents do not happen – they are caused'. Similarly, mistakes are caused – usually by human actions. Since we cause them, we should accept responsibility for trying to avoid them, or at least for rectifying them as speedily and efficiently as possible. When errors occur, it is because:

- the design is faulty, (so design out the problems);
- the execution is faulty, (so improve quality control);
- the service is faulty. To the average consumer, this kind of error is the most irritating since, frequently it is the most easily avoided.

The director of a major conference and publishing house recently told me that he estimated the prime cause of most of the problems with their customers to be errors resulting from computerisation. Whilst it is true, if trite, to point out that computers only very rarely make mistakes, since the mistakes are usually related to errors of programming software or systems (all the responsibility of humans), often it may be the responsibility of the computer salesman assuring the client that the machine can do something that it cannot. The mistakes here are then caused by an inadequate specification or failure to comply with that specification.

The effect, however, is that in each case the customer provides good value and the supplier does not. It is not surprising, having parted with value and found the goods or services lacking, that customers become demanding and frustrated such frustration often finding an outlet in anger. The supplier is actually the prime mover in generating the dispute, a point often overlooked when a response is required.

28

Case study 3.1
Misrepresentation

The owner of a small business was approached by a major source of business advertising to insert an entry in a directory. The business already ran two advertisements but suffered from the fact that it was located on the boundary of two directories' areas. In resisting the representatives urging, the owner explained that the cost was not inconsiderable to his size of business and since the company needed him to place the order nearly 18 months before the directory would be published, he was uneasy about such an additional commitment. The representative stated quite clearly (and the statement was witnessed and noted at the time) that 'you can cancel the order any time before the invoice is due'. On that basis the order was placed.

Circumstances changed and when the invoice was received the owner returned it, cancelling it, referring to the statement made by the representative. There then developed a dispute with the company refuting the statement made by its representative. Eventually the company backed down and cancelled the invoice.

> **Remedial action**
> Brief representatives strictly regarding what they can and cannot say.
> Require representatives to draw the attention of the customers to written

terms before commitment, or confirm these terms (in plain English) on an Acknowledgement of Order slip issued within a few days of the order being placed.

Case study 3.2
What else do you expect?

In 1993 an employment case went to the Court of Appeal. A representative was paid commission on insurance policies he sold. Thus his income was generated by his convincing members of the public to buy a policy. One policy he sold was felt by the company to be entirely inappropriate for the individual concerned and as a result it dismissed him. The employer and the employee were required to work under strict guidelines which the employee had breached in making the sale.

Remedial actions

(1) Review very carefully the rationale behind the whole basis of payment that encourages this kind of problem. A higher base and lower commission might avoid this kind of problem by removing some of the pressure to perform that tends to lead to shortcuts.

Recently Marks and Spencer has announced that it is to sell pensions through its financial services subsidiary. Interestingly however, the financial advisers selling the policies are all to be salaried, receiving no commission or incentive on what they sell, presumably to avoid the problem underlying the above case.

(2) Ensure automatic supervisory review of all contracts with client check-back facility in the event of any doubt.

(3) Withhold commission until supervisory clearance is given.

The problem of employers lacking control over statements made by their representatives (particularly those who work entirely on their own) will be addressed in more detail later. However, the underlying point of both these case studies is that the problems were caused partly by the suppliers setting up systems which seemingly had the effect of pressurising employees into making statements, later disowned, in order to get the business. If the income of employees depends on them obtaining new business, particularly in a recession when such new business may be difficult to find, it is hardly surprising if those at the sharp end bend the rules. After all, they will argue, the chances are that the person will not be able to remember what was said. The losers, when someone makes notes or has a good memory and challenges such statements, are the suppliers themselves, whose reputation and profits are damaged. In March 1994 the *Financial Times* reported that Legal & General were fined £180 000 (and had to pay £220 000 costs) for failure to keep proper control of its direct sales agents, and particularly failure to ensure those agents complied with the self-regulatory authorities guidelines.

Staff stability

COSTS ARE INCURRED

In case study 3.1 the situation was aggravated, as far as the customer was concerned, as the company suffered from high labour turnover. Thus each time the original order came up for renewal, either a different person dealt with it or the situation was complicated by two or three representatives telephoning, and apparently competing, to take the order. This confusion became so great that on one occasion the customer threatened to cancel all advertisements his businesses were running unless one person was able to deal with them all. The company's system (or more accurately, lack of policing a system) was itself in danger of becoming the prime reason for the aggravation of, and creation of a demanding customer, and eventually a potential loss of business. The point that high employee turnover tends to lead to greater customer dissatisfaction bears repeating here.

Few suppliers seem to appreciate that having exchanged value for goods, the customer does not expect to have to pay further. Yet if the goods develop a fault or there is faulty service, then usually the onus is on the customer to telephone or write, or perhaps make a special trip back to the outlet with the faulty goods. Either way he incurs further costs to try to obtain satisfaction.

Case study 3.3
Deserving of decoration

On entering the room the day after hanging the wall covering, the customer was horrified to find that one drop from the second roll she had used was a different shade despite the shade numbers being the same. Quickly removing it from the wall, she opened another roll only to find that it had a flaw in the design. She made a special trip to the DIY warehouse to explain the problem. In replacing the faulty rolls the company also gave her two additional rolls, all from new stock, partly to ensure a more than adequate supply, partly to compensate for the trouble caused, and partly for the time taken 'to drive back here'.

Key technique
That customer recounted this incident, praising the store, to many acquaintances. The cost of the rolls of wall covering to the store was negligible – the potential adverse public relations had the aggravation not been recognised was considerable.
Remedial action
Ensure there is a guideline to assist front line staff as to what action to be taken where it is not a simple replacement of a faulty product but the customer has suffered inconvenience and/or loss as a result of their purchase.
Warning
Sadly it has to be noted that experience shows that a proportion of customers will seek to abuse such a policy and such attempted fraud does need to be guarded against.

If recognition of the point that costs are incurred simply in raising a legitimate complaint is not forthcoming, then, almost inevitably, further aggravation will build.

Case study 3.4
Gaining no credit

The retired customer was concerned that a cheque made payable to him did not seem to have been credited to his building society account. On visiting his local branch, they advised him that they could not deal with it and he would have to 'take it up with Head Office'. 'But that's 300 miles away' he remonstrated 'why should I run up costs telephoning them when it is your mistake?'

Remedial action
The assistant could have offered to phone the Head Office on the customer's behalf or put a note from him about the complaint in the Society's internal post system.

Customer respect

The essential ingredient missing from many of these adverse encounters, is that of respect for the customer and his or her position. In case study 2.3, to the bored telesales girl, the person at the other end of the telephone was presumably another annoying interruption to her chatting. Similarly the assistant in case study 3.4 showed no concern for the customer or interest in the possibility of his having to spend his own funds trying to sort out her society's mistake. In both instances, the result was to aggravate the situations rather than solving them. The building society assistant may have been acting in accordance with guidelines laid down by the society. If so, the society itself was showing that it had no respect for its investors and, should this become widely known, could well pay the price of this dismissive attitude, after all its 'product' is essentially substitutional. The suppliers that accord respect to their customers tend to acquire and build a positive reputation, those that do not may also acquire a reputation – a negative one that may damage the organisation.

32 Taking the initiative

Retailers and those providing services like banks, building societies and estate agencies where a public interface is almost inevitable must provide training for every employee. This may not be essential for other organisations, even though it may be valuable to encourage all employees to think like salespeople. All those directly involved need to be trained:

- to listen carefully;
- to encourage customers to reveal their problems; and
- to try to keep calm no matter what the provocation.

The slogan should be 'we cannot put right what we do not know about' with the rider 'tell us and we will see what we can do to rectify the situation'. Provided these watchwords are always to the fore, most problems should be resolved fairly easily.

Research in the USA indicates that 94 per cent of people want to get along with each other, and, by extrapolation, will be prepared to accept a sincere apology possibly backed by a nominal compensation or restitution. That leaves only a 'difficult' 6 per cent of the population to contend with. This sounds a nice manageable number until you realise that 6 per cent of the UK's 56 000 000 population is over 3 million people who, if American research is to be believed, can become demanding! It should be obvious that our prime goal should be to draw the sting from all complaints as quickly as possible to avoid as many as possible moving from the 94 per cent to the 6 per cent. Strangely, this is a strategy totally ignored in many of the case studies cited, yet for want of a swift apology and nominal compensation, low profile skirmishes were often turned into potentially far more costly battles.

Case study 3.5
No real help

The customer was extremely concerned that many items in his post seemed to take much longer than the time claimed by Royal Mail for delivery. Accordingly he began monitoring his post noting postmarks and delivery times and gradually built up research showing that the 'next day delivery' claimed for 1st class post was not being achieved.

He sent copies of the envelopes to Royal Mail who investigated the situation and, after being reminded, eventually produced some statistics stating that the number was very small. The customer replied that it might be a small proportion but multiplied by the number of outlets for post in the UK it indicated that a massive number of letters posted first class were not being delivered the following day.

The correspondence continued in a desultory way, some letters not being dealt with for months at a time. Royal Mail produced further statistics but, as the customer stated with increasing irritation, 'what I want from a customer service department is an improvement in the service not a load of statistics.'

Key technique
It seemed to the customer that all the customer service centre was doing was answering correspondence courteously enough but without entailing any action that would actually **improve** the situation. As he once commented 'I really fail to see the point of your operation'.

Remedial action
A customer care operation must be provided with the scope to actually compensate for or correct problems (or both). Going through the motions with sympathetic attitude and correspondence may simply aggravate the situation.

Designing out the problem

In considering designing out in this instance, we are not so much concerned with the design of the product or service, as with preventing the incidence of complaints which in turn will help negate their impact and enable us to deal with them adequately. Mistakes are often caused by human error and in all of our procedures and practices we need to check the human interface and minimise the adverse effect that carelessness can cause.

Case study 3.6
Treat the customer like royalty

The philosophies of the Stew Leonard store, founded by its owner of the same name, are that:

(1) 'Shopping should be fun': the store employs mechanical displays as well as a range of cheerful entertainers – animal and fairy tale figures – based on the Disneyland concept, who constantly circulate, amusing customers' children.

(2) 'If you take good care of your staff, they will take good care of the customers and of the store': employees are paid double normal rates, and over-achievers (who tend to be the rule rather than the exception) are constantly rewarded. Employees' commitment to the store and the service concept is considerable.

(3) 'Keep it simple': the average USA food store stocks over 20 000 items – Stew Leonard stocks only 800, but every item is fresh, stock turn is considerable, and the customers love the service, value and freshness concepts.

(4) 'If you take good care of your customers, your customers take good care of you': the emphasis is on value and price being passed on to the customer. The store sources its goods predominantly from the producer, rather than from a wholesaler. The fact that a customer makes only a small purchase each week does not reduce their value in the perception of the store – '$50 spent each week amounts to $26 000 over a ten year period and the customer should be regarded as a $26 000 not a $50 customer' is the approach.

Stressing the long term nature of customer and supplier – so that the $50 a week shopper is treated as if at that time he or she were spending the full 'long term' $26 000 – emphasises to the employees the necessity to ensure that good customer service is provided and that each customer is taken care of to the limit of their ability.

This attitude may be far more common in the USA than in the UK.

Case study 3.7
'You're selling them a Cadillac ... not booking a vehicle service'

Carl Sewell runs a Cadillac dealership in Texas and has calculated that a long term customer with him could spend around $330 000 on a combination of servicing and replacement cars. The customer will only become 'long term' if he or she is satisfied. 'Once you realise a sale is not a one-off transaction then it makes sense to keep the customer happy.' This entails asking customers what they want and then providing it. Thus he extended his opening hours and also provided a free replacement car for use whilst a customer's car was being serviced. In addition he makes his customers 'feel good' by giving estimates for servicing, which include a built in 'price buffer' of around 10 per cent so that the bill always comes in under the estimate.

(See *The Golden Rules of Customer Care*, Sewell and Brown, Business Books.)

Key technique
Asking customers what they want may be a valuable exercise in public relations, but it must be backed up by an intent to incorporate some improvements. If not, expectations will have been raised, and the subsequent failure to attain such expectations will damage the relationship. In other words if it is intended only as a public relations exercise, forget it, it would be better not to ask.

Arguably if there is no possibility of any repeat business being derived from a customer, a less caring approach may be feasible, but one should never underestimate the power of publicity which can be generated by a customer who feels he has been poorly treated. Satisfied customers may talk, but dissatisfied customers talk loudly, widely and often, as did the guests concerned in case study 2.1, initially between themselves during their stay but then to others when they returned home. To misquote the old phrase 'hell hath no fury like a customer scorned'.

Customers used to the 'service with a smile and value' ethics of the likes of Stew Leonard or Carl Sewell must find it disturbing to deal with those without such standards. As noted previously, if we do not maintain the standards shown by those at the 'cutting edge' we will compare unfavourably. This comparison would be particularly marked in comparing US and UK goods and service as UK goods tend on average to be almost twice as expensive as those in the US.

Case study 3.8
Getting a poor press

The advertiser 'phoned the newspaper to gain a quote for, and to place, a classified advertisement. The cost calculations were quite complicated and thus in the order letter which quoted a credit card account in payment, the advertiser limited the amount of the payment to his calculation of the cost. An acknowledgement of the order was received with no query as to the price he had calculated, but when the advertiser received his credit card statement he found it had been debited 50 per cent more than his authority. On writing to the paper, his first letter was ignored and so he sent a reminder to the Chairman of the company and also contacted the credit card company. A letter was then received from the paper, which sought to place the blame on a part-time member of staff who had not replied 'as she had no means of reply'. A complaint was lodged with the credit card company.

Key techniques
(1) Blaming a junior member of staff is hardly fair, but if it was her fault, then stating she had 'no means of reply', when she had used the phone to take the details, merely showed the paper's staff to be ready to lie. A telephoned apology and explanation would have defused the whole encounter and allowed the full charge (if correctly calculated) to be collected.
(2) Trying to cover up merely annoyed the advertiser so that he was determined to 'show up' the paper to the credit card company. Whilst the latter would probably not take action on a first complaint, were more to be lodged the paper could find themselves delisted, which could severely damage their ability to take advertisements over the phone – as well as their credibility.

Remedial action
Issue an acknowledgement of order which confirms the correct price, and if incorrect payment has been received politely request either further funds or an additional/replacement authority.

Putting oneself in the customer's place will be examined in greater detail in Chapter 8. Unless we understand why the customer is complaining and his desired result, it is unlikely that if we will be able to manage the encounter successfully.

Case study 3.9
A better solution

In case study 3.4 the society handled millions of deposits and withdrawals each year. Despite the greatest care we are entitled to assume that it takes with such transactions, it is perhaps expecting too much that they could all be effected without an occasional hitch. Had it recognised this, the society could have either provided an external free telephone number for depositors with such a problem, or provided a telephone connected to Head Office within each branch. If even this proved too difficult or expensive, since it is reasonable to assume that Head Office does contact its branches occasionally, use of the branch phone could have been allowed, even if strictly controlled.

37

The right respondent

In case study 3.8 it is arguable that part of the problem was caused by the fact that the person who dealt with the reply to the reminder letter was probably not the best person to do so. The customer had addressed his letter to the Chairman and could feel slighted if he did not at least receive an acknowledgement from the Chairman's office in terms such as are set out in Figure 3.1.

Receiving such a letter should mollify the most difficult customer and 'buy' a little time for consideration of the problem. As a further devel-

---

From the Chairman's office

Dear
We thank you for your letter of [date] addressed to [Chairman's name]. He/she is sorry to learn of the problems set out in your letter and has asked [name] to look into the situation and to reply on his/her behalf within the next [number] days. [Name] appreciates your bringing this matter to our attention and stresses our commitment to resolving your concerns. Yours sincerely

---

Figure 3.1 Chairman's holding letter

opment, it may help if the letter can actually be signed by the Chairman. This device can help to calm the irate and sooth the aggravated. However that is only the start of the process since it is then essential that some positive action is taken within the time limit set. Failure to do this will set the whole process in a worse environment than before the acknowledgement was sent.

If solving the problem is delegated it must be to an appropriate person – one with the experience to consider the problem and with the authority to 'make a deal'. If the person left to do the deal has no such authority and has to keep referring back to gain agreement, this may be a source of aggravation which can turn a drama into a crisis.

Case study 3.10
Redundancy

The Group Chairman wished to remove the Chairman of the subsidiary company and instructed the group secretary to inform the Subsidiary Chairman that he was to be made redundant and to negotiate terms. The secretary checked all the details of the proposed severance package that he could offer and made an appointment to see the Subsidiary Chairman. Whilst the latter listened with interest to the package the secretary outlined, he brought the interview to a premature end by asking just one question – 'Why am I being made redundant?' Neither could the secretary answer this question nor was it his place to do so – the Subsidiary Chairman reported to the Group Chairman and it was the latter who had to take the initiative. He could legitimately delegate the agreement of the package but not the delineation of the reason for termination – that was abdication of his responsibility.

Key technique
The net effect of the meeting was entirely negative. The organisation had disclosed its hand as far as the package was concerned but in using a more junior person than that appropriate for the task, merely aggravated an already difficult situation.

Remedial action
Ensure the right person deals with the problem to ensure that the situation is not aggravated merely for want of investment of a more senior (or appropriate) person's time.

38

4

On good terms

Key learning points

1 Terms of business must be clearly promulgated and understood by all.

2 Jargon should be avoided in the interests of clarity and customer rapport.

3 Control must be exercised over those who have the ability to dilute the effect of terms.

4 Other bases of our business need to be examined to ensure that our desired image and the customer's perception of us do match.

Getting the fundamentals right

The fundamentals referred to here are the terms by which we carry on trade with our customers – the basis of the contract between the two parties. Getting these terms wrong is simply inviting trouble. It seems unbelievable that having gone to such an immense effort setting up a business, investing time and money in an idea or process and developing contacts or generating demand for our products, the essential need to establish the means by which we should generate the income of the business which is the sole purpose of the whole endeavour, should then be overlooked. However, many businesses do make the mistake of not devising, promulgating and adhering to purpose designed terms, thereby unnecessarily creating demanding encounters – and demanding customers.

Profitability depends on customers paying up, so we need to ensure that the basis on which we trade is clearly defined, and known by all. Our position, trade and assets will then be protected and our customers will know what is expected of them. If we are without terms we lose the ability to ensure our customers pay us correctly, and are entirely lacking in protection from the unscrupulous.

Case study 4.1
The customer is always wrong

This was the second order placed by the customer. The first had been a somewhat rushed order for Christmas gifts and the second was in response to a discount flier the company had produced to try and generate trade in the low demand part of the year. Following its standard practice, the company had produced and invoiced 10 per cent over the number of items ordered. The customer telephoned to query this.

'I am very surprised to see that the order which I requested for delivery by 1st April was delivered late without any apology and in addition you have charged me for overs.'

'That is in accordance with our standard conditions of trade shown on our catalogue – I'll send you a copy.' (1)

After receiving the catalogue, the customer telephoned again.

'I queried your charging for the overs on my second order, and the late delivery, and you have sent me your catalogue. However, I would point out that your discount flier makes no reference to any such conditions. In addition, you have ignored the fact that the order was delivered late, even though I had stressed in my order that the date was critical and you did not query it on your Acknowledgement of Order form. However, in re-reading the catalogue you have sent me, I have also realised that you overcharged me for my first order last Christmas, as you charged for the overprinting which is not referred to as being a charge for the goods I ordered.' (2)

The matter was passed to a director.

'We are sorry to hear you are unhappy with the company (3a), our offer sheet was rushed out and we overlooked the requirement to refer to our terms, and we will be mindful of this in future to avoid any such remote misunderstandings (3b). We enclose a credit note for the cost of the overs. Do accept our unequivocal apologies for the late delivery, which under any circumstances should not have occurred (3c). You are correct in identifying a discrepancy in our catalogue. Unfortunately this was noticed after the printing had been completed, but it was felt our customers would appreciate that even though it does not state this, the additional charge would apply (3d). We feel it is unreasonable of you to stress this point (3e). We hope that with this explanation you will feel more sympathetic towards us and the efforts we make on behalf of our customers (3f).'

'I note all that and accept that mistakes do happen, but when they do, the correct course of action is for the company to accept responsibility, not to try to evade it.'

'But there was no deliberate attempt to mislead you – yours is the only query that has been raised regarding the charge for overprinting – and we feel it is unreasonable. We would appreciate your settling our account.' (4) & (5)

Key techniques

(1) Treating a genuine customer query in this dismissive way, as well as ignoring one of the points raised, merely stores up trouble for the future. Here, had the supplier realised there was a problem with the terms, it could have offered a credit note for the overs and saved itself the £50 eventually deducted from the outstanding invoice.

(2) Further, it was only the irritation caused by the dismissive approach which was the direct cause of the customer investigating further. Now the company had to either try to justify the three matters, or to negotiate (rather than impose) a way out of it.

(3) This dismissive response seeks refuge from the facts in unnecessary and totally 'flowery' wording, the effect of which is merely irritating. Plain language without jargon, flattery or 'flowery' phrases is preferable and more effective. In addition the comments slide round the facts – the customer had a genuine grievance which, despite all the words, has not actually been answered. He was not unhappy with the company (3a), but he is unhappy with its unprofessional service, particularly as he is being forced to waste time trying to sort out its mistakes. This makes the last comment (3f) utterly illogical. Since it is the customer who has suffered – why should the company (3e) expect sympathy? By its own admissions (3b, c & d), the company is in the wrong in each case.

(4) This is a response which could work although there is considerable risk of it coming unstuck. No-one has stated the mistake was deliberate, whilst reasonableness is an opinion which the two parties are unlikely to share. Whether the customer believes his was the only query is irrelevant – it is a real query and a real overcharge to him. Further, the onus and the power is now with the customer regarding the settling of the account. If he fails to settle at all, the company could take legal action to recover, with all the attendant inconvenience and costs (which in the circumstances it is unlikely to recover), but it does leave the customer the option of deducting the disputed amount from

41

the account when settling it, which would then place the onus for further action on the company. Conversely, the customer, since the order has been acknowledged as being delivered late, could insist that the company take the whole order back, which is the last thing it would want.

(5) The company failed to appreciate its goal and lost sight of the desired result. The result should have been satisfaction of the customer when raising a legitimate matter of concern, and avoidance of a returned and wasted order. A more sympathetic and positive approach initially would have saved a great deal of time, trouble and eventually a deduction of funds.

Remedial actions
(1) Never send out promotional literature containing a material error. Whilst reprinting may be uneconomic, a correction slip or label can avoid uncertainty and loss.
(2) Promotional literature should always refer to the appropriate terms of business – a note 'Standard terms of business apply (available on request)' is sufficient.
(3) Having been caught out, come clean. Trying to cover up merely makes the company look devious, whilst the majority of customers respect the truth. Justification is pointless and an apology far more effective. The French phrase is most apposite 'qui s'excuse, s'accuse' (whoever excuses themself, accuses themself).

Case study 4.1 displays the shortsightedness of trying to defend an indefensible position with the sole effect of increasing the customer's annoyance. However, more importantly, it also demonstrates two further points:

1 How a relatively minor problem which should have been easily rectified with little cost can develop into a major and public row. The customer was so annoyed that on receiving the company's brochure for gifts for the following Christmas and finding the same mistake repeated, he reported the company to the local Trading Standards Office.
2 The critical necessity of getting one's terms of trade right and indeed of abiding by them, if we are to reduce the incidence of occasions when we have to deal with demanding customers and indeed if we are to have a solid foundation for putting our own case across in any dispute. Had the wording on the flier referred to the standard terms to be found in the catalogue, the customer would have had to accept

the charge for 'overs'. However the flier bore no such reference, indeed it bore no terms at all, and it was reasonable to assume that you would pay only for what you ordered and not 10 per cent more than you ordered merely at the whim of the supplier. That may be one way of increasing trade but presumably at the expense of repeat orders! Under domestic laws likely to be required under the European Union's Unfair Contract terms directive, it is unlikely that such a charge for 'overs' would be considered fair and recoverable at all.

Terms to be written and read

As long as the company complies to the letter with its terms, if restitution is requested by a customer beyond those terms, the company will have every right to resist claims. As a natural corollary, it can be argued that one way of avoiding conflict or the creating of difficult encounters, is to ensure the terms of trade are:

43

1 WELL WRITTEN

Terms should be framed using decent everyday English, particularly if dealing with private consumers who cannot be expected to understand the pseudo-legalistic phraseology often used. British Telecommunications (BT), the UK's largest company has recently revised its manner of communicating its terms to its customers. The vast majority of BT's customers are private individuals who are unlikely to want, or be prepared, to read, let alone understand a 'typical legal document comprising line upon line of formidable jargon and very little interesting reading' (from BT's Conditions for Telephone Service February 1994). Similarly 'contract' is a word which has undesirable and legalistic overtones to many people, so BT calls the document an 'agreement' which is a far softer sounding concept giving inferences of consensus and joint approach. In addition BT's terms have been re-written in ordinary English so that they are easy to follow and understand. What BT have achieved is to make their terms 'user-friendly'. If BT's millions of customers can now read and understand the terms under which they use the company's products and services, it should save misunderstandings and thus resources. In addition, most of the jargon which tends to confuse the uninitiated has been eliminated.

Case study 4.2

The wrong box

The home-based business had been sold and the old telephone number trans-
ferred with it. The customer asked BT to supply a new number, the order for
which was handled very promptly and the engineer duly attended on the following (bitterly cold) Monday to carry out the changeover. Having climbed the telegraph pole and worked there for 10 minutes, he came into the house and said
to the householder 'Where's yer box?' For a moment the householder thought
he was asking for a cricketing device to protect him from the extreme cold of the
telegraph pole, but then reasoned that he did not need to rummage in his aged
cricket bag and what was needed was a telephone connection box. He pointed
out the box on the window sill where the line entered the house. This however
was not the required item – what was needed was the small plastic holder into
which can be inserted the plug on the end of the cable attached to the telephone itself.

> **Key technique**
>
> Using jargon may save time if those using and receiving it both know what is
> meant. With those who do not know, jargon merely confuses and annoys –
> and fails to save time, since that time must be spent explaining it.
>
> **Remedial action**
>
> Train staff interfacing with the public to be specific about items they need or
> to which they refer. The customer is not expert in the subject matter, the
> engineer/salesperson/representative should be. Patronising or attempting to
> baffle the customer can rebound spectacularly. The customer may not be an
> expert in the subject matter but they may be expert in obtaining compensa-
> tion or restitution if they feel they have been poorly treated.

2 BROUGHT TO THE ATTENTION OF THE CUSTOMER

Terms need to be brought to the attention of customers before purchase, that is before there is any commitment. It is unreasonable and
simply invites demanding encounters for a supplier to produce, when
a customer complains about a widget that he bought three weeks ago,
a set of terms in complex language in which lies buried a comment
that states that the expected life of the widget is 96 hours from purchase. Terms must be displayed adjacent (in the widest sense of the
word) to the purchase.

3 KNOWN AND UNDERSTOOD BY THE EMPLOYEES OF THE SUPPLIER

Those who will have to interpret the terms must know and understand what they are discussing.

Case study 4.3
Arguing on the wrong foot

Having advertised regularly in a magazine for some years, the agency was advised that the owners of the magazine had changed. Subsequently, with trade being badly affected by the UK recession, the agency decided to suspend advertising for two issues and received the following reply:

'We note that you wish to suspend your advertising. Since you are cancelling your advertisement, I must advise you that there will be a cancellation charge and in addition, you will be required to repay your series discount.' (1)

In telephoning to query this, the conversation ran as follows:

'But we have never agreed any terms with your company.'

'Yes you have – the terms state that late cancellation leads to a 25 per cent charge and cancellation of a series leads to repayment of the series discount.'

'I am sorry but I must disagree – you are referring, incorrectly, to the terms issued by your predecessors. No terms have been issued by your company.'

'For the pittance of commission I am paid I am not going to provide new terms for the one instance where an absence of goodwill leads to this kind of problem.' (2)

'That is completely irrelevant. Normally this would be a question of contractual commitments, but in this case there is no formal contract. However, leaving this aside, even if we accept your predecessor's terms, they do not set out the charges as you have indicated. Only if there is late cancellation is there a charge, and although one understandably loses the series discount, those terms do not indicate that the customer must repay the discount obtained earlier.'

'You have cancelled late.'

'I am sorry, but I cannot accept that – we told you of our decision more than six weeks before publication date.'

'We need to know six weeks before copy date.'

45

'But that is not what your predecessor's terms state – they refer to six weeks before "publication date". I gave you notice over three months before one, and over six months before the other publication date.'

'Well, we rely on the goodwill of our customers and I don't accept this kind of close analysis of terms.'

'But the terms govern the contract, and besides it was your analysis of those terms which led to this discussion. That analysis was totally incorrect – hence our querying it. I repeat that we gave several months notice of suspension of our advert, having advertised every quarter in your magazine for several years. As a customer of some long standing I feel we are entitled to better consideration than that evidenced by this conversation.'
(3)

Key techniques

(1) It is unlikely that this can be accepted as the best method of communicating with a long term advertiser and customer!

(2) Angry frustration may be understandable, but is not going to solve the problem, it will merely aggravate the situation. Seeking to obtain sympathy as a technique seems curious, but is surprisingly widespread. It is rarely effective.

Remedial actions

(1) Issue terms and update as and when appropriate.

(2) Train staff to be familiar with terms and to abide by them in the event of dispute – at least initially. Obviously there may be a need for flexibility in some instances.

(3) Avoid becoming emotionally involved in confrontations.

Basically if a supplier's staff are to debate, discuss or rely on terms then it is essential that they:

- have complete understanding of such terms.
- quote the terms actually applicable, and
- quote their terms correctly.

Losing one's temper, no matter what the reason, will almost certainly result in losing the argument. Far better, if 'caught on the hop', as she was, to say, 'sorry there seems to have been some misunderstanding here, I must consider this and will come back to you.'

Terms control

Thus, to minimise our need to deal with demanding customers we need to address the basic way in which we undertake our business, take orders and fulfil those orders. The following guidelines demonstrate how a number of problem areas can be eliminated by getting the rules right, as well as reducing the need for the company to chase payment by restricting the incidence of those who can abuse the system. The illustration assumes the supplier is a manufacturer operating with a sales force. Although much of the wording and procedure should be replaced for other situations, the principles and general intent will be very similar.

MAKING THE SALE EFFECTIVE

1 Representatives (and/or Agents) must comply with the agreed journey-plan and submit their call report schedule within five days of the end of each accounting period.

2 Deviation from price list values may only be permitted with the prior written authority of (name of authority). (1)

3 Details of proposed orders being variations from the standard list, showing number of units, delivery date, etc., must be submitted to (name) who will advise whether the variation can be produced and, if so, the price/delivery to be quoted. (2)

4 Complete details on the company's official order form must be shown. The customer must confirm the order by signature and retain a duplicate copy. The status of the signatory should be checked to ensure he/she has appropriate authority. (3)

5 Orders below the minimum order level (specify: cash/product numbers) will only be accepted on the basis of a *pro forma* invoice (ie payment being made with the order) which will bear a minimum handling/delivery charge. (4)

6 Orders from new customers will be accepted, but not processed until receipt of two satisfactory trade references, and credit clearance.

7 Sales staff are expected to liaise with Credit Control to set a level of trade which seems reasonable given the customer's financial standing. Orders in excess of this level may only be accepted with the prior written authority of (name).

8 Journey cycles and terms of trade means payment for an order placed in month (x) should have been received by the next call but

---

one. Finance department will advise if this is not the case so that the representative/agent can investigate the position.

9 Subsequent orders will not be processed until payment is received. The order acknowledgement will bear a warning that repeated poor payment will lead to a requirement to use the *pro forma* system or to a suspension of supplies.

10 If difficulties are experienced with payment, visits by Sales and Credit Control staff will be made.

11 If it seems that a customer is in financial difficulties this fact should be brought to the attention of (name). (5)

12 Terms need to be carefully delineated, regularly updated and brought to the attention of the customer, either prior to the effective date (where a change has been implemented) or on the first placing of an order. (6)

Key techniques

(1) Orders that deviate from price lists, apart from involving the possibility of destroying margins, can generate disputes where customer A, paying the full price, discovers that customer B is gaining the benefit of an advantageous price. Logical reasons for the difference are essential to combat the inevitable complaint.

(2) Similarly, variations from the standard product, which are likely to be more apparent than an advantageous price, may not only reduce profitability but also prompt demands from other customers for similar bespoke products or for a price reduction for taking the standard product.

(3) & (4) Most supplier/customer disputes revolve around costs and charges. It is essential that the whole basis of the order and its authority is clear from the start.

(5) Early notification of this event may enable action to be taken at an early stage to avoid the worst effects.

(6) Notifying and keeping the customer up to date regarding terms and changes should avoid complaints of the 'I didn't know variety'.

Figure 4.1 'Getting the terms of business right' checklist
(Part Two of this checklist will be found in Chapter 13.)

Avoiding trouble

It is not just a question of getting the 'legal' terms right, but of ensuring correct comprehension of the terms and/or the basis of the contract between the parties. If subsequent checking discloses incorrect perceptions and misunderstandings, these need to be addressed. In delivering several presentations every year at seminars and conferences on a number of management subjects, one often becomes aware of a difference of perception between the parties, which can often generate demanding customers.

Case study 4.4
Reading between the lines

'The speaker did not cover the subject matter' – 1

In fact the speaker kept exactly to the programme laid down, but often around 10 per cent of delegates attend without having seen the programme. They are sent by a superior who has determined that they should attend. However, the delegate at the course is the customer and his or her needs need to be met or this kind of backlash can be created

49

Remedial action

A copy of the course brochure is inserted in the delegate pack and referred to on the day. This gives an indication of the subjects to be covered, making it even more crucial that the subject matter is covered.

'The speaker did not cover the subject matter' – 2

Not quite correct – he did cover the subject-matter but not within the context expected by the delegate. The problem here was that the speaker had not been properly briefed by the organisers and he concentrated on a sphere of activity parallel to that of the delegates.

Remedial action

The specification to the speaker must correspond to that which generates the target audience. The reaction to the comment must be either:

– to try and cover the mistake by apologising and attempting to make amends by supplying data on the area of interest overlooked, and/or

– to actually come clean and explain the reality of the mistake. My preference would be to use the latter, as the danger with a cover up is that it can be exposed as just that, in which case the result is worse than it was in the first place. Obviously mistakes do happen and telling the truth about them, in an age when often this is an exception, may enhance rather than damage one's reputation.

'The approach was too-lighthearted – these are serious matters.'

This is very subjective since what one person will find light-hearted another may find quite heavy and in the average audience there is bound to be such a cross section of tastes that one speaker's style of presentation is unlikely to appeal to all.

Key technique
Once again the approach to be employed should be stressed in the originating documentation, and to avoid the point already made about some delegates not seeing that documentation, ensure that the point is repeated in any brochure issued on the day. Some humour is valuable in these situations since not only does it help relax delegates (we tend to absorb more when we are relaxed), but also an occasional laugh draws oxygen into the lungs and body and refreshes us which in turn re-awakens us. The latter is a particularly valuable device in the post-lunch session when traditionally delegates can be overcome by drowsiness! Obviously speakers should be instructed to ensure that if they use humour this should not have the effect of trivialising the subject matter or the delegates themselves.

Intention mismatch

If the incidence of complaints is high we must examine the basic perception of what is on offer, to discover why suppliers' and customers' intentions do not match. Intention mismatch is the inevitable source of many demanding customers and awkward encounters.

5

DARNing the holes

Key learning points

1 Those interfacing with customers, at whatever level, must be adequately trained

2 Basic procedures need to be devised and constantly policed.

3 Complaints should be welcomed since from them we can learn how to improve.

4 Customers provide invaluable feedback on our products and services in the marketplace.

Nothing will undermine more our genuine commitment to customer service than a failure to train those who deal at the sharp end. We really must ensure that we have the right staff to deal with the problems that arise and that they are;

■ trained to an appropriate level

■ provided with the requisite equipment to perform the job, and

■ given managerial support where necessary.

This cannot be undertaken swiftly since product knowledge, which takes time to assimilate, is as important as knowing how to handle complaints and customers. Further, with a fast moving business, there are usually fresh versions of old products or entirely new products with which those responsible for converting customer complaints or 'courting the customer' need to familiarise themselves. The aim must be to demonstrate to customers that the 'dealing-employee' knows the subject and the process and understands the problem. Nothing creates frustration more swiftly than to find that the person responding is ignorant about the product – not only does the problem need to be explained but so too may product details.

Case study 5.1
Waste of time

Within a few days of the installation of new kitchen units including a 'pop up' plug for the drainpipe, the connection between the 'pop up' control and the plug itself ceased to work and water was found to be leaking from the pipe. The joint (presumably from the time of installation) was 'made' by the pipe being jammed between the drain and a strategically placed shelf.

On ringing the installation company to explain the problem the only person the householder could speak to was a young receptionist who obviously only had the haziest idea of what the company for whom she was working actually did and had even less understanding of kitchen sink connections. An explanation of the function of a 'pop up' waste having failed to penetrate, the householder gave up and told her he would fax a sketch showing what he thought the problem was. 'What's a fax?' came the reply.

Needless to say, the owner of the company, when he rang back, received a somewhat cooler reception than would have been the case had someone who knew the product and recognised the problem dealt with his enquiry.

Key technique
In allowing an untrained and ill-equipped employee to 'deal' with a customer the business had created a demanding customer where none had existed.

Data collation

The receptionist's problems were three-fold:

- she lacked product and office system knowledge;
- she lacked training in complaint handling, and
- she was put on the spot in terms of a response.

The first two of these can be dealt with only by continual training. The last should generate an instinctive response. Very often, those interfacing with problems feel forced to respond in a way which, on later reflection, they may consider to have been unwise. If circumstances allow, it may be preferable to consider complaint processing in two or three stages the first of which is purely 'data collection'.

52

'Good morning sir.'

'I want a refund for these shoes.'

'I see, sir, can I just take a few details first? If I can get all the facts down, I will pass the details to our customer care department and they will get back to you within 24 hours.' (1)

'I just want a refund.'

'I understand that, sir, and if we can get the details, we can arrange to process any refund due within 24 hours – now could I have your name and address, sir.' (2)

The conversation continues with the assistant collecting all the relevant data, possibly on a purpose designed form. In this way the complaint is reduced to its essentials.

'If you would just leave that with me sir, I will ensure someone gets back to you within 24 hours with a refund if appropriate.' (3)

'It had better be appropriate.'

'We will do everything we can to accommodate you sir. Do you wish to leave the shoes, in which case I'll give you a receipt, or would you prefer to hold on to them?' (4)

'But if I leave them with you – I'll have lost my evidence.'

'You still have your receipt sir and I am going to give you a copy of the notes I have taken on which you can write a description of the state of the shoes, if we give a refund we will wish to hold onto the shoes in any case.' (5)

Key techniques

(1) The prompt and efficient approach should impress most customers.

(2) The assistant tries to defuse the anger by asking a neutral question.

(3) This indicates the next step and how long it will take. Having indicated that it will be 24 hours obviously an answer must be given within that time, or the situation will become aggravated.

(4) This gives choice back to the customer whilst point 5 should provide reassurance that the customer will lose nothing by leaving the items.

By using such a procedure the supplier generates data on the complaint as well as evidence of the source of the problem. It can now calmly decide the appropriate course of action to take. Divorcing the data collection from the eventual deal may not only reduce the length of the encounter but should also restrict the propensity for both sides to misunderstand the other. The two have different aims – one is trying to get the facts, whilst the other is trying to gain recompense, which the former cannot grant without the facts!

53

Fig. 5.1 Complaint data collection

It is unlikely, were it just a simple matter of a refund on a pair of shoes, that one would use such a process. It is more applicable to a high value transaction. However, where specific details are essential and the question of whether a refund is appropriate or not must be determined, adopting such a procedure may be effective. Even then such a procedure may not work with a really demanding customer and it may be necessary to refer a customer to a supervisor, or experienced employee, to defuse the situation.

Recording the data

Inherent in the suggestions included above is a wish or intent to minimise the effect or inconvenience caused by such mistakes. Such an attitude is vital if we are to ensure that those who have a query can have it answered swiftly and efficiently without aggravation.

Case study 5.2
Got it taped

By chance, when it opened for business one day, the agency left its ansaphone switched on and the first call was taped. This call was not from a customer, but from a relative of the customer who had received a garbled, and erroneous, message, from the customer herself, and, somewhat foolishly, had decided to take action on the basis of such information, including giving the complaint publicity to a third party. Simply because, by accident, the agency had the message taped, it had:

- time to consider how best to rebut the erroneous accusations, and
- evidence in her own words of the action the relative had taken.

Having time to consider and reconsider alternative responses, when not under pressure, is very valuable, as instinctive reactions can be unreliable and, once uttered, words cannot be recalled. 'Members of the jury kindly disregard that remark' is an understandable and laudable comment but one entirely impossible to achieve, indeed by commenting on it the original item may be even more firmly fixed in one's mind.

Thinking twice

The concept of drafting or framing a reply and then sleeping on it, to give time for reconsideration is very valid, and echoes the old story of the Medes and the Persians who were reputed to make decisions twice – once when drunk and once when sober! Whilst not recommending imbibing before dealing with customers, the idea of double consideration is valid. Too often the immediate response to a problem or complaint is 'send a standard letter'. Standard letters are fine and can save a great deal of time and resources. However it is essential before using them that consideration is given to the question 'is this a standard query?' Obviously if the query is not standard and inevitably some will not be, then not only is the standard reply inappropriate, but sending it may actually convert a simple complaint into an aggrieved demand for proper consideration of the point made. This reaction parallels a similar attitude – the inability to read correspondence carefully and to answer the actual question posed, or to ignore a request made. Organisations that fail to insist that all correspondence is read carefully do themselves or their reputations few favours.

Case study 5.3
Check carefully

When paying my monthly credit card account I noted a request that cheques being placed in the envelope should not be folded although the cheque issued by the same bank as that operating the credit card company, was too big to be placed in the envelope without folding! I suggested to the credit card company that they increase the size of their envelopes. A standard reply was received that their envelopes were able to accommodate standard bank cheques.

I pointed out that they obviously had not checked the size of the cheque sent with the note as, even though it was one of their own cheques it still needed to be folded. They checked with the bank who stated that appropriately sized cheques were available.

When ordering a new cheque book, I requested such a cheque book. This request was ignored – indeed the letter did not even receive a reply, so I am still folding the cheque. Some people you simply cannot help!

DARN

A further advantage of data collation referred to in Figure 5.1, is that detailed information is in a form capable of being stored and available for reference. In this it can provide the last step in the process of

DARN. The process of darning is to repair and make as new, and this is the underlying message of the mnemonic in this context. Here DARN stands for Discovery, Apology, Rectification and Novation. By getting the facts down the supplier discovers the problem which should generate an apology or learns more about the product which may help its development. This is part of the theory behind the use of 'carelines' referred to in Chapter 2. From the data, subsequent consideration of the problem should lead to rectification, whilst recording aspects of all complaints and problems will build a data bank that should be invaluable to management in terms of 'novation', that is setting up new procedures, checks, designs and so on, to avoid repetition. For this reason it is recommended that details of all complaints should be regularly reviewed by senior management. If data on such problems is not reviewed and acted upon, there is little likelihood that common problems will be rectified and the incidence of demanding customers will almost certainly increase, at the expense of the organisation's reputation.

Customer satisfaction

Few sizable organisations can operate without someone to handle customer complaints. Having such an appointee or department should be regarded as a positive sign of commitment to satisfying the needs of the customer. To overcome any inference that it is necessary to have someone to handle complaints 'because the service/products, etc., is/are poor' the title 'customer complaints' is best avoided. Although descriptive, the word 'complaint' is emotive and inculcates in most people an immediate and defensive position, which is not the reaction that we wish to achieve any more than it is indicative of the approach that we want our staff to adopt. A report of a faulty product or service should be seen as the supplier's opportunity to:

- create a rapport with the customer. UK research indicates that although 40 per cent of dissatisfied customers will repurchase from the same supplier despite its former failings, where their complaints have been rectified, the number of repeat customers rises to 80 per cent.

- rectify a mistake. In the USA, research for the Technical Assistance and Research Programme (TARP) for the White House office of consumer affairs discovered that businesses do not hear from 96 per cent of their dissatisfied customers – for every complaint received, 26 customers have problems and six have serious problems.

- minimise inconvenience and repair the damage before the news spreads. TARP discovered that customers with bad experiences are twice as likely to tell others as those who are satisfied. A person with an unsatisfied complaint is likely to spread the news widely – 'hell hath no fury like a dissatisfied complainant'.

- reconsider systems, designs, attitudes, etc., mainly in order to avoid repetition, but, more importantly, to improve quality. Gaining market research direct from customers in this way is a cost-effective means of developing and improving products and service.

Case study 5.4
The opportunity in the complaint

Many suppliers only speak to a customer when there is a complaint, yet customer rapport is very valuable. Thus the complaint situation needs to be viewed as an opportunity firstly to convert a complaining customer into a satisfied customer and secondly to create a rapport that hopefully will result in repeat custom. As Colin Ringrose, Managing Director of training course providers Popular Communication put it 'We welcome customer complaints. They show us what we are doing wrong so we can put it right, and, in doing so we may get the chance to sell the customer something else'. This is converting customer complaints at the sharp end and seizing the opportunity of direct customer contact as a learning encounter for the positive benefit of both parties.

The description 'customer care' or 'customer satisfaction' creates a positive ambience, rather than a negative one, and indicates at the outset that the company really wants to help.

Satisfying the right customer?

Underlying the more obvious lessons included in many of the examples highlighted is the vital need to ensure we have the right customer for the product, as much as the right product for the customer. If we are aiming a product or service at the wrong customer then the propensity for complaint will be high – as in case study 4.4. Conversely, if there are insufficient 'right' customers for our product, then it is futile to 'buck the trend'. As we cannot change the customers, we need to change the product, as Sir John Harvey Jones comments in 'Managing to survive' – 'Your business is only as good as your customer base.' This is not meant to imply that we should only seek to satisfy compliant customers. Indeed one tends to learn more from those who tell us what is wrong than we can ever do from those that praise us. After all it is the person who refuses to accept poor quality, poor standards or poor delivery that is the one source that can actually guide us to where we are falling down and help us improve all three.

In case study 2.1 only one guest actually complained to the hotel about the poor standards and was able to guide the management's attention to those points that he and a number of other guests, who had simply voted with their feet to rival hotels, had felt were unacceptable. If the source of the problem is not told of the problem then nothing is likely to be done about it. Here not only were customers disappointed, but competitors were assisted – a vital point often overlooked. There is usually a replacement supplier only too glad to take the custom we disappoint. Thus there is a logic in encouraging complaints – albeit trying to insist that they are of the constructive variety.

Indeed, if we wish to survive, we **must** hear from the non-compliant as their constructive comments should help keep us on our toes. If they force us to improve our act so that we satisfy the demanding customer, then we should have it made, as satisfying the others should be a doddle. If the demanding customer does not tell us what is wrong and simply does not patronise us again, they may have lost out but far more importantly so have we. As a supplier we:

- have no information as to why we did not satisfy that customer (which may mean we will continue to lose others);
- have lost a customer who could have given us valuable information about the perception of our business and our products in the market place;
- now need to replace that customer simply to maintain the *status quo*, and
- have aided our competitors.

'Go west young man'

As noted in the earlier examples of the attitude of the Stew Leonard and Carl Sewell businesses, American attitudes to custom and customers are generally different to those in the UK. Consumer and market power, the need to satisfy, and the real and constant competition makes US suppliers far more aware of the need to serve the customer. 'Serve' is used here in the widest meaning of the word. In some areas of UK business, the concept of 'service' conjures inappropriate images of 'subserviency' and perhaps because of this in some instances tends to be resisted. Because we are an island race, geographically and historically separated from a continent and by language from our nearest neighbours, and by oceans from those countries that use the same language, this can lead us to become insular in our attitude. Most of our suppliers tend to be small, competing for the most part with other small suppliers. As we try to compete in world markets, we find ourselves in competition with much larger rivals some of whom will be setting standards which we must emulate, in markets where consumers expect high standards. Only if we can match or exceed those requirements will we win – or even survive.

59

Case study 5.5
Benchmarking

Traditionally, when it came to their cars, Americans simply 'bought American' and although a few foreign manufacturers managed to penetrate the American home market mostly the vehicle trade was driven in the reverse direction with American cars finding their way into most countries in the world. However, when barriers against Japanese cars were reduced, the American public found that these new imports provided better value, performance and all round quality than many of their home produced models. Swiftly Japanese cars producers seized a large slice of the US car market. There was only one way to combat the threat – US manufacturers had to improve their standards to match.

Key techniques
(1) Comparing one's own performance against the best produced in the market place – or benchmarking – and achieving such standards, should entail being in tune with the most demanding customers' expectations. Maintaining this level of performance in turn should reduce complaint incidence.
(2) 'Respected' here is used deliberately since if the competitor is taking our market and our sales, they need to be respected – even if thoroughly disliked!

Gaining feedback

There is an additional value in companies making a positive effort to encourage customers to notify them when there is a problem. Not only are they then learning what their customers feel about them and their products, but they are also drawing the sting of such complaints in the first instance. This tends to be the normal manner of approach in parts of Europe and in the USA, where customer service is seen as a priority. However, in many instances in the UK, customer service and the satisfaction of complaints is not given such positive response. Since the average consumer knows that if he raises a complaint the expected reaction will be defensive, and that he will need to fight to gain rectification of the 'damage', many duck the challenge and vote with their feet. Realisation that only a small percentage of those who may be dissatisfied will actually voice such concern is extremely important, as these complaints may be indicative of a far more widespread problem. If we have such a problem we should want to know about it – fast.

Policy required

To offset UK consumers' reticence about complaining, suppliers may need to encourage customers to contact them whenever there is something wrong. If this is the policy, the commitment should be displayed boldly as part of a separate Customer Commitment, not buried in a mass of legalese in the terms of trade. If the terms have been translated into decent English it may be possible to include it there but either way its import must be brought to the consumer's attention – like the 'carelines' referred to in Chapter 2.

Board responsibility

Tom Peters, the American management guru identifies:
- a willingness to flatter its customers;
- a consciousness of the importance of service, and
- a high degree of responsiveness to market requirements,

as the three most important factors that will help organisations become what he describes as 'winning companies'. To achieve these three factors it is essential that organisations speak to their customers and deal with their problems and complaints effectively.

This cannot be effective unless backing up the sharp end operators – those who initially have to field the queries and complaints – are senior managers who do not just deal with awkward problems, but are able to recognise trends and common factors and correct mistakes. It is also vital that they in turn are backed by a board level policy commitment. Giving board responsibility to the customer care or customer satisfaction function grants it a prestige and creates awareness amongst other parts of the operation that quality and satisfying the customer are all important aspects of their job. This is where the buck, as far as customer satisfaction, really ought to stop, with the decision makers, not with someone like poor 'bored voice', paid a pittance to sit at the end of a phone,

- sans training
- sans knowledge
- sans understanding
- sans, in fact, everything she needs to cope with her difficult task.

61

Case study 5.6
Premier retailer's promise

Arguably Marks & Spencer's most widely-known claim to fame is its undertaking to replace or provide a refund for unwanted goods bought in its stores. Inevitably such a policy must be abused by some customers, nevertheless the company is famous for the practice. The fact that, virtually without quibble, an item can be exchanged must result in considerably increased sales, the profit on which, no doubt, comfortably exceeds the losses incurred by those who abuse the system.

Case study 5.7
Boxing cleverly

The customer bought several packs of Christmas cards and found two envelopes missing in each of three of boxes. Since he had some spare envelopes he was not unduly concerned but on revisiting the shop advised another customer to check the number of envelopes before purchase. A supervisor overheard the comment and asked for further details.

Immediately she opened another pack and handed the customer eight envelopes, partly to replace the missing six and partly as an acknowledgement of the information. The customer related this story to many acquaintances.

Key technique

The cost to the company of the envelopes was negligible – the value of the customer's goodwill was perceived to be substantial.

The Marks and Spencer customer appreciation and refund/replacement policies operate throughout the company's stores in the UK and entail virtually every employee knowing their principles and practice. Where customers interface with employees, the latter must be trained to deal with them positively – and indeed trained to serve and help them properly. It is not servility it is civility – and it pays off. It is also noticeable when absent.

Case study 5.8
Service without courtesy

In visiting the local Building Society, the depositor was always irritated to find that when dealing with his business, one particular assistant continued talking to other assistants and also called out to other customers as they came in. He pointed out to her supervisor that this was not only extremely bad manners, but also distracting and could lead to mistakes being made

---

Key technique

Presumably, never having been taught that talking to someone else whilst dealing with a customer was bad manners, the cashier involved did not realise how discourteous some customers would find her attitude.

The Policy Commitment

Whilst a procedure for dealing with customers should attempt to cover most eventualities and would, one would hope, ensure that the discourtesy outlined in case study 5.8 was avoided, the Board needs to create an appropriate ethos within the organisation by means of a policy commitment.

BLOGGS COMPANY LTD

CUSTOMER RELATIONSHIP POLICY

As a wealth-creating organisation our aim is to make a profit by producing products and/or services which are of value to our customers. Organisations do not stand still – they either expand and prosper, or contract and ultimately go out of business. We wish to expand and thus need to be able to satisfy more customers each year, or at least to obtain more income from our existing customers each year. To achieve either (or both) we need to satisfy those customers with value, quality, delivery, etc., and expect all employees to bear the following commitment in mind at all times:

1 We commit ourselves to produce quality/value products available at the time required by the customer.
2 In the event that a problem arises with a product, we will endeavour to deal with such a problem objectively and positively, with the aim of both solving the problem and converting a dissatisfied customer into a satisfied one (see Chapter 7).
3 Complaints. All complaints, no matter what the source or basis, will be treated with courtesy and a positive attitude. This is so even if it means compensating a customer where there is no genuine complaint, or where a complaint seems to be exaggerated.
4 Customer visitors will be treated courteously and, provided the time is appropriate, invited to tour the premises (except for any parts of the operation from time to time considered as sensitive or secret which will be suitably protected).

63

Figure 5.2 Draft company customer service policy

Fostering an appropriate ethos

Adopting policies that will encourage and ensure positive consumer contact sets out a commitment to adherence to a practice which must be communicated through the whole organisation. Thus everyone should know the commitment, should realise how it affects them and should realise how they are expected to comply.

Case study 5.9
Three thousand sales representatives

Endeavouring to motivate employees to improve quality and productivity and reduce inefficiency, the director made two suggestions. Firstly, that all 3 000 employees consider themselves salespeople, even if they never saw a customer, in order to encourage awareness that everything attempted ultimately led to a sale, and secondly that all employees realised that the company's customers paid everyone's wages and it was only through the company satisfying its customers that it was possible for wages and continued employment to be provided. Analysis of production subsequently revealed that returned product fell from 10 per cent to 4 per cent, whilst a survey of customer satisfaction showed a corresponding rise. As one employee said 'I only thought in terms of getting the products to the stock room, although I suppose I knew that thereafter someone had to sell them and someone buy them, it never really dawned on me that I was part of that process or that the money the customer handed over was for these products I was handling. When I realised that I handled everything far more carefully.'

64

Key technique
Involving staff in order to generate a link between shop floor and customer aids both the perception of the problem by those targeted as well as its ultimate accomplishment.

6

Dealing

Key learning points

1 Dealing means 'reaching a settlement' not 'discarding' and can restore the damaged reputation of the business.

2 Assessing the cost of rectifying complaints may provide food for thought.

3 Failing to carry out what has been promised aggravates the whole situation.

4 Many demanding encounters are caused by an inadequate response to an initial passive enquiry.

Removing the source of aggravation and making amends in a relatively minor way may actually solve a large proportion of demanding encounters. Left unanswered or subject to rectification delays, such problems can snowball and change annoyance to anger and frustration, and an annoyed customer into a demanding customer. The offer of a credit note or monetary recompense is sometimes regarded as a sign of weakness which can be exploited, and a slow approach regarded as helpful to 'deter others'. It is certainly true that precedents can be dangerous and be quoted against the supplier, however they can only ever be a guide and do not automatically need to be followed. Of course, even admitting that something could be used as a precedent infers that one is anticipating further complaints of a similar nature which must say something about the standards, or lack thereof, in business performance. Using the American research, 94 per cent would probably be happy with an immediate and nominal settlement, whilst only 6 per cent would use the offer as a weapon to try to get more. If the problem is related to one of the 6 per cent, they would probably be going for broke in any event, so having an immediate offer turned down by them is little real loss and the chance of acceptance would be well worth taking.

Deal rather than delay

When referring to dealing with customers, we may be trapped into using the word 'deal' in a dismissive context, that is in the context of being 'dealt with and discarded'. However it may be far more constructive to consider 'deal' in the context of 'doing a deal', that is making a bargain acceptable to both sides, but possibly entailing concessions from **both.** After all, if the customer has a complaint about a product or service then, assuming it is justified, he has a case for restitution from the supplier. Restitution here could entail replacement of the damaged or faulty product but could also mean compensation in respect of losses consequential to the failure.

66

Case study 6.1
Head crash = parties clash

The retailer had bought a computer system, one of its selling points being that it could process much of the input overnight and provide a data printout when the office and warehouse opened the following morning. One night, whilst running unattended, the computer had a head crash, shorted out and caused a small fire. Fortunately, it happened at a time of the year when there was a twilight shift working in the warehouse. The fire was spotted and swiftly extinguished. The computer company maintained that their terms stated that they could not be held responsible for any consequential damage caused as a result of a machine failure. The retailer refused to accept this, pointing out that the rationale for using the particular system, indeed the inference under which the system had been sold, related to the fact that it could process information overnight when the office was unmanned. The retailer was no expert in computer systems and had not appreciated, nor had the computer company made it clear, that should the system fail in the way that it had it would not 'fail safe' but could cause damage.

After considerable argument, during which the retailer refused to commit to a further order for an additional machine, the computer company agreed to replace the damaged equipment and to make a payment towards the repairs and redecoration. A deal was done.

> **Key technique**
> It should not be overlooked that if there is a continuing relationship with a customer, it may be difficult to hold a particular line for risk of losing further business. Dogmatic reactions should be avoided, a pragmatic and holistic view of the relationship needs to be taken.
>
> **Remedial actions**
> (1) Ensure the terms say what they mean, mean what they say and are fair.
> (2) Explore the reality of each situation. Situations are rarely black and white and solutions may have to be 'grey compromises'.

In case study 6.1 the sums involved in terms of all the repairs were not large. The potential profit on the sale of the additional system was much greater – as indeed was the potential downside in terms of adverse publicity and public relations to the computer company. Such an adverse publicity dimension can be a major cause of loss to some companies.

67

Case study 6.2
Doing a deal

The holidaymakers had hired a canal boat for a holiday in France.

The boat, which was glowingly described in the brochure, turned out to be somewhat less appealing in reality. It also had a habit of breaking down, which it did three times, meaning that instead of cruising, the holidaymakers were forced to wait for a mechanic to reach them, thus effectively wasting part of their holiday and curtailing their enjoyment. Since the mechanic commented that 'it was always happening with these boats' the holidaymakers felt this to be unacceptable.

On their return the holidaymakers put the problem to the cruise company which initially dismissed the complaint out of hand. Since it seemed to the holidaymaker that the company had made no effort to understand either the loss caused by the breakdowns or the deleterious effect this known unreliability had had on their (and presumably other people's) holidays, he wrote personally to the Chairman of the company.

The following Sunday morning he was impressed to receive a telephone call from the Chairman of the company who apologised not only for the unreliability of the boat but also for the dismissive way his initial letter had been treated. He went on to ask how they could put the damage right and it was agreed that a discount on a future holiday with the company would be appropriate.

> **Key techniques**
>
> There were a number of advantages to the company in this method of handling the problem:
>
> (1) A personal telephone call showed how seriously the company took the complaint.
>
> (2) The fact that it was the Chairman himself who made this call on what would normally be regarded as a non-working day added solace to the 'injury' caused by the initial dismissive reaction. The company was seen to have 'put itself out', compensating in some degree for the way the holidaymakers had been 'put out' by the breakdowns.
>
> (3) The positive publicity given to this initiative had a disproportionate public relations value to the costs involved.
>
> (4) The fact that a deal was done over the telephone meant as far as the company was concerned there was nothing in writing which could be quoted back to them as a basis for trying to increase the amount or used as a precedent by others.
>
> (5) A deal was agreed between principals without what could have developed into a long winded correspondence which could have had the effect of further polarising viewpoints.
>
> **Remedial actions**
>
> (1) Train and empower customer care employees to suggest flexible solutions to problems either themselves or by referral to supervision.
>
> (2) Try to do the deal verbally – it saves time and avoids the permanence of print.

Getting a good deal

In seeking to come to a swift conclusion it must not be overlooked that trying to conclude a disagreement by correspondence is far more difficult than doing so either face to face or on the telephone. When words are reduced to black and white text they lose all tone and inflexion, and can acquire a stilted formality. Conversely, the tones and inflexions we use when speaking, both soften and give otherwise 'hidden' meanings to their literal meanings. This is impossible when we write. Written communications lack eye and voice expression, indeed all body language. Furthermore, we have to use words which may have different and unwanted meanings to different people which can create or compound misunderstandings. Put simply – one cannot ask questions of, or elucidation from, a piece of paper. There is also a tendency, in composing a letter, to get 'carried away' with the 'correctness' of our views and case (another reason for leaving a draft of a letter for later reconsideration before despatch). In a conversation, our flow would be interrupted, either by voice or by bodily reaction, and such interruption might give us pause to think again and possibly modify our response. This does not happen when we write – we cannot determine or even second guess exactly how our words will be taken. Finally, writing has a permanence which a conversation does not. In case study 6.2 the Chairman seeking to do a deal over the telephone had several advantages over his colleague who had answered by letter:

1 He could tell by the tone and attitude of the holidaymaker if he was likely to be amenable to a swift deal.
2 He could check out the facts and gain an impression of the strength of the case being made.
3 He could float ideas during the conversation with a reasonable degree of confidence that much would not be recalled accurately and, if difficulties developed, could even be denied.
4 He could try to conclude a deal without any written offer being made.
5 He could use verbal pressure to gain agreement.

In fact the conversation was more the result of an instinctive reaction – genuine sympathy for a holiday somewhat spoiled and a wish to agree some recompense swiftly. It was also relatively easy for the Chairman to arrange a deal in view of his complete authority.

Written dealing

In contrast the situation outlined in case study 6.3 shows how polarisation can occur when a dispute that could have been solved by telephone or personal visit was instead mishandled by post.

Case study 6.3
Meeting better than writing

A customer had a major query with a building society's product and service and had written to the local branch to gain information and redress. Over the following two months a number of letters flew backwards and forwards, the situation being aggravated by the branch making a number of further minor errors which only served to worsen what was already a difficult situation. Inadequate and insufficient explanations were provided and eventually the customer involved the Head Office at Board level. As a result a further three way correspondence ensued which continued for several weeks.

When the situation was to some extent sorted out, even after compensation was paid, the customer was left feeling that he had been inefficiently and poorly treated. In terms of customer care this was hardly an encouraging outcome, whilst in terms of potential adverse publicity it was dangerous.

Key technique

A meeting between the customer and a senior person in the company who could have investigated the original problem and the subsequent mistakes the society had caused, checked all the details, agreed action and ensured proper restitution, might have achieved a better and swifter solution.

In this instance, such a meeting would have had the advantage of the recognition of body language, was unlikely to have degenerated into dispute and would have had the advantage of not providing a written record of the maladministration. The time invested in such a meeting would have avoided the potential downside as well as the resources consumed in a lengthy and at times acrimonious correspondence which reflected well on no-one, least of all the building society, for which one would think a sound customer-orientated image was essential.

Remedial action

Adopt as policy – if the problem cannot be resolved by an initial letter, a telephone call or visit from a senior member of staff should be used to attempt resolution.

Whilst it has been said in criticism of meetings that they take minutes and waste hours, on occasion, the time consumed in the holding of such a meeting can be extremely beneficial and may save time and use of alternative resources. The decision making process can take several forms and one or more means of solution may be acceptable. What is required on every occasion when a problem arises is the commitment to an objective assessment of what the best solution is likely to be, rather than an automatic assumption that writing is best. Of course, if setting up a meeting it is essential that the participants meet!

Case study 6.4
Losing out

The customer was experiencing a number of annoying aggravations and demanded that the items be attended to. Instead of dealing with the items over the telephone, the supplier suggested that he come over to their offices to discuss the problems and to meet the new manager who would be handling his account. He arrived at the time stated and was kept waiting in reception. Having twice asked the receptionist to remind the contact that he was waiting, he was eventually seen 20 minutes late. However, on enquiring after a further 10 minutes where the new manager was, he was told that he was unable to make it. 'Fine' was the reply 'in that case I shan't place next year's contract with your company.'

Key technique
Even if not intended, the 'message' conveyed to the customer was of complete disdain and a lack of respect. Consequently his reaction was that, having undertaken a round trip of 140 miles, he could treat the supplier in the same way. The encounter was a typical example of how to create a difficult customer where none previously existed.

Interfacing

Regardless of whether verbal or written means are used, the protagonists will need to communicate. No decisions, discussions or deals are possible without real communication, which is one of the most misunderstood words in common use. If A meets B and complains that the widget he bought from B is faulty he may feel he is communicating with B, but this is not so, he is merely informing him. Although information is essential, in no way does it involve B, or gain any commitment from him. However, if A contacts B, tells him the widget he bought is faulty and asks him what he can do about it, and B then answers, possibly requesting further information before making a decision, he has begun the communication process. If he then actively listens to, not passively 'hears' A's further comments, and then A and B jointly decide a course of action, communication is in process and is helping to attain the joint ends of the participants' interfacing. True communication consists of a meeting of minds and a gaining of consensus. It is essentially a two-way dialogue involving comprehension of both parties' viewpoints, concerns and priorities, which can only be achieved by an **exchange** of information and feedback. It is a dynamic, not a passive, process affecting all parties as is shown in the following illustration.

	INFORMATION	FEEDBACK	COMMUNICATION
Sender:	I	F	C
Data encoded	N	E	O
Transmitted	F	E	M
Received	O	D	M
Decoded	R	B	U
	M	A	N
Recipient:	A	C	I
Received	T	K	C
Decoded	I		A
Comprehension	O		T
Clarification	N		I
			O
			N

Figure 6.1 Information =/= communication
(from the author's 'Manipulating meetings – how to get what you want when you want')

Using a meeting

In attempting to conclude a deal, a face-to-face meeting, as an alternative to a telephone call, or worse, lengthy correspondence has a great deal to commend it. Eye contact and body language are important and cannot be substituted for on the telephone, although the advent of videophones may well change this view! But there are other advantages, particularly to the instigator of the one-to-one meeting. If we assume A instigates a meeting then:

(1) A has control of the discussion and the subject matter. He has his aims firmly in view, but must accept that in order to achieve them he must convince B of the value of those views.

(2) A, one assumes, having taken the initiative, will be prepared for the encounter and thus has a better chance of manipulating his desired result than B who may be forced to react without advance planning. In fact, B might be wise to request time to consider the proposal before committing himself.

[3] A also has control of the tactics of the meeting and can decide time, place, duration and so on. He can also consider arranging matters so that a deal can be contrived without B losing face, or manipulate the conversation so that his own desired suggestion for resolution appears to emanate from B, and so on.

Costing the deal

One advantage of using the telephone or face-to-face encounter when trying to conclude a deal, apart from speed, is that the reaction of the other party to the suggestion is more easily gauged than is the case in correspondence. This is important as it is in the interests of the organisation to provide a deal which seems reasonable to the other side. Make it too mean and it may encourage the customer to return for another bite. Make it too generous and it may create a precedent. Unfortunately there are some who will try to gain compensation for a case no matter how weak or questionable. Compensation which entails the company's products or services may be ideal here since the perceived value to the customer is usually far greater than the actual cost to the supplier. It also helps draw the sting of the complaint should it be repeated elsewhere, particularly if publicity is given to the deal. After all, if a complainant has agreed to take further supplies in compensation for a complaint, any suggestion that the company's products are poor, fails.

As already noted, however, there are far more costs involved than just the restitution and the longer it is before the deal is concluded the greater the costs involved – hence the recommendation to try a kind of pre-emptive offer, one that settles the dispute at an early stage, before management time is committed to trying to resolve what then tends to become an increasingly polarised dispute. The form set out in Figure 6.2 seeks to force consideration of all aspects of the costs involved in resolving complaints.

COMPANY NAME Complaint Ref....................	COSTS
CUSTOMER DETAILS Name .... Address... Tel. No................................Ref.	 Basic
PRODUCT DETAILS Description... Reference number... Purchased	 Reputation
COMPLAINT DETAILS Advised on (date) By Person/Telephone/Letter/Other (specify) Nature .... Restitution required	 Aggravation
ACTION DETAILS Investigation... .... Supplier/Engineer comments.. Customer comments .... Other	 Time Travel Admin.
RESTITUTION DETAILS Suggestions .... Accepted.. Authority..	 Recompense
RECTIFICATION REQUIRED Specify .... Action by (state name/position and date required) .... TOTAL ERROR RECTIFICATION COST	 Improvement
Reported to Board ....(date) .... Approved..............(Initial)	

Figure 6.2 The cost of the problem

Explanatory notes

The content of this form should be reasonably self-explanatory, although the various headings/information queries need to be customised for individual use. The assessment of the various categories of costs needs some explanation. The following figures are inserted for example. Some of these may seem high but research indicates they are not unrealistic

Basic: Every complaint wastes resources before it is recognised as such and should bear a charge of (say) ...   **£10**

Reputation: The fact that there is a complaint against the organisation damages our reputation, and entails us in expense in restoring our good name. A notional charge needs to be allocated to each complaint. This is for individual consideration and may depend on the seriousness
of the complaint. For the sake of example ...   **£50**

Aggravation: Each day that the complaint is unresolved aggravates the complainant to the extent that further and more public notification of the complaint may be engendered. A daily charge of at least £10 should be made. If we assume the complaint will take 20 days ...   **£200**

Time, Travel and Admin.: Complaints absorb management time – and if not resolved swiftly and competently tend to absorb the time of more senior management. Allowing for all oncosts and benefits as well as salary, the charge for the Chief Executive could total £1 per minute, with proportionately less for more junior personnel. We will take an average charge of 50p per minute and assume that it takes around 180 minutes to deal with the average complaint ...   **£90**
(Note that this assumes a reasonably swift settlement
If there is a dispute this figure could be considerably increased.)
All travel costs need to be reflected should an on-site inspection be required, or the customer needs, or be requested to travel to the organisation, etc. In addition, letter writing, telephone, computer input, as well as all oncosts involved (heating, lighting) should be costed against the complaint. All are being incurred whilst the organisation is dealing with a complaint and not furthering its business. For an average complain ...   **£40**

Recompense: Obviously this depends on the product or service under complaint, but on the basis that most people will not complain about something worth less than (say) £20, that could be a minimum
figure ...   **£20**

This gives a total cost to be borne by the supplier of ...   **£410**

Such a cost speaks for itself and the fact that many of these costs are hidden should be no consolation. The form also allows for consideration of rectification of errors so that, should the complaint be likely to recur, advance action can be taken, whilst it also calls for the Board to authorise the action not so much for the actual granting of authority to commit resources to the problem as to ensure that the body likely to wish to take action are advised of the problems arising.

The right treatment

Trying to minimise expenditure on correcting errors and problems can be achieved by encouraging customers to contact the company. Subsequent resolution of such problems may make good public relations copy, but only if there is adequate back up will the real value be realised. Sadly, there often seems to be a vast gulf between those responsible for creating the image of the company and those seeking to ensure that the practical implications of that image are dealt with. If the company promises to deal positively with problems then an essential ingredient is the establishing of appropriate systems to deal with the problems in the manner and to the standard outlined. If, having advised everyone that the company wants to hear from its customers, the actual manner of dealing with such contact is faulty, the result and the possible increased aggravation can be far worse than if it had not suggested it wanted to hear from them in the first place – so will the costs incurred.

Case study 6.5
Adding insult to injury

The holiday company advertised in its brochure that at the end of every holiday it invited all holidaymakers to complete a questionnaire on its service, arrangements etc. On their return one family spent some time completing this questionnaire in detail. Their holiday had been good but its complete success had been marred by a number of shortcomings all of which were entirely the responsibility of the tour company. The family amplified the questionnaire with a letter complaining about these shortcomings. As no answer was received within a month, and the holidaymaker was a shareholder in the company, he felt sufficiently aggrieved to write a personal letter to the Managing Director pointing out that ignoring the letter of complaint, let alone the import of the matters raised, when the company was on record as stating that it wanted to hear from customers, merely added insult to injury. Virtually by return came a holding letter apologising and indicating that a full investigation was in process and a week later came a letter acknowledging the truth of the complaints and offering a cheque for around 15 per cent of the total costs.

Key technique

The holidaymaker accepted, pointing out that, whilst as a holiday-maker he found the offered deal satisfactory, as a shareholder he was not at all happy that a letter outlining a number of complaints had not received proper consideration, and that those responsible need-ed to be taught to understand that such incompetence could easily lose customers, thus threatening its own profitability.

Remedial actions

(1) All correspondence to be acknowledged within 24 hours (vital with this kind of personal service organisation) and answered within 15 days.

(2) Non-standard replies to questionnaires to be passed to manager for immediate attention.

Creating the demanding customer

In several instances of poor complaint reaction already highlighted, people who were simply customers with problems were converted into demanding and difficult customers purely because of an inadequate initial reaction from the supplier. The fact that this needless aggrava-tion of a situation is totally self-defeating seems to have escaped the attention of the suppliers' representatives involved. The inadequate reactions involved have included:

- poor response;
- late response;
- dogmatic reaction;
- failure to appreciate the other side's viewpoint;
- unthinking response;
- patronising response and so on.

Not only could all of these have been easily avoided and the initial problems solved with relatively little attention, but the failure to solve the problem in the early stages, led, in each case to a situation where the encounter became far more difficult, consumed far more resources, including both time and money, and very often resulted in a potentially reputation-damaging conflict. The fact that customers do talk to other customers simply does not seem to occur to many of those who are responsible for dealing with such problems, yet in May 1994 Syd Pennington, Managing Director of Virgin Atlantic, commented 'If someone has a bad flight he is likely to tell 17 people'. Whilst a failure to do a deal at an early stage for fear of precedent-creation can be understood, all too often what transpired had nothing to do with that and was more related to inadequate systems, inadequate training and inadequate respect for the vital importance of the customer. All are essential concomitants of the process whereby we try to do a deal.

7

Sharp end SARAH

Key learning points

1 The aim should be to convert complaints into extra sales, and complainants into repeat customers.

2 Listening to customer complaints will help defuse aggravation.

3 Customer complaints should be monitored at Board level to ensure full appreciation of costs, problems and any cover-ups.

4 Positive reaction to complaint situations is essential.

Whilst the drafting, approval and promulgation of a 'satisfy the customer' policy commitment is a relatively straightforward task its implementation is not, nor is that implementation a once and for all task. Companies, systems and products constantly change, and so too will the type and range of customer queries and the information required to enable those at the sharp end to implement the practice. Further, the composition of those dealing with customer queries will constantly alter, requiring newcomers to be trained.

Bloggs Company Ltd

CUSTOMER COMPLAINTS CONVERSION – CCC

Policy

Our operation is geared to satisfying our customers since it is only through satisfying our customers and more of them that we can pay for everything on which we spend company money, including our own wages.

It is our policy to positively encourage contact with customers so that:
1 The company obtains feedback from the market place – since

unless we know pricisely how the market place views our products we cannot develop and improve them.

2 Problems and queries related to our products and services are brought to the company's attention for rectification.

3 Positive customer satisfaction is generated with both our products and our after-sales service.

4 CCC has several functions:

- to create a rapport with the customer and market place;

- to discover the true nature of problems;

- to discuss/decide any contribution to any loss suffered;

- to attempt to retain the customer for repeat sales;

- to preserve the company's reputation, and

- to consider whether it is necessary to implement any design changes as a result of the information generated.

Practice

Training. Every employee who may come into contact with customers will attend the 'CCC' training course before being placed in a position of customer-interface. Such training will include product and organisation familiarisation, principles of customer care and negotiation, inter-personal skills, guidance on levels of authority and so on.

Initiation period. Having completed the course an employee will remain under the guidance of a supervisor who will be able to provide advice and guidance during an initial period of work.

Refresher. Every six months thereafter all 'CCC' department personnel will attend a refresher course.

New products. All 'CCC' personnel will receive briefing on all aspects of every new product, and will be provided with technical data, brochures etc., to ensure that they become conversant with the item.

Figure 7.1 Customer complaints conversion policy

SARAH

The people who are required to actually deal with the customers need every assistance and comprehensive training to ensure the policy adopted finds a true outlet in practice. Hence the detailed and ongoing reference to such training. The principles of good customer relationships can be summed up in the process described by the mnemonic SARAH. SARAH is a friendly and helpful export from the USA and, although she was originated more for use in selling, her principles apply equally to customer negotiation. SARAH contains five key aspects.

*S*top talking: if the supplier's employee is talking the customer cannot be heard and nor can their complaint. Nothing riles customers more than for the other party to keep talking, preventing them explaining. It seems that an attempt is being made to 'talk out' the subject matter.

*A*dopt active listening: the corollary to ceasing to talk is to listen more. This means much more than hearing what is said. Hearing is purely a mechanical act, whereas listening entails active consideration of both what is said and what is left unsaid.

*R*eflect content or feeling: to show that the employee has understood what the customer has said they should repeat key sentences or comments in their own words. This has three advantages:

- it helps fix the details of the problem in the mind of the employee;
- it helps check that what has been received by the employee was what was meant by the customer; and
- it engenders a rapport between the two which can be used as a base for a settlement.

*A*ct with empathy: this entails showing that the employee understands and appreciates the feelings and motivation of the customer. If empathy and perception (see Chapter 8) are lacking, customers will conclude that they are wasting their time as the organisation does not really care about their views.

*H*andle the subject matter: most complaints concern overcharging, faulty products or services, or failure to meet a deadline. These are real problems and the customer is very much the injured party. The organisation has responsibility to correct and possibly compensate and the deal must be done in that light.

Implementation

Speaking at the 'People mean business' conference organised by the Local Government Board in autumn 1993, Sylvie Pierce, chief executive of Reading Borough Council told delegates how she had given receptionists at the council the power to decide whether members of the public could see the council officers. Implicit in this move was a recognition of the importance of the receptionist's role as the public face and voice of the organisation, and the fact that such staff would need to be aware of the scope of responsibility of each executive, and the potential importance of the business wishing to be transacted. 'You have to identify the key people in the organisation – and for me these are the receptionists,' she said, 'you never get a second chance to make a first impression'. The knowledge and training provided in order to make this kind of move work requires considerable investment in people.

Managing the process

At Reading Borough Council the lead was taken by the Chief Executive encapsulating the need for such decisions to be taken by top management. Quality of product or service should be one of the prime considerations of the controlling body of an organisation. Sales, indeed the whole survival of the organisation, is bound up with the meaintenance of a level of quality commensurate with the value demanded for the item. Despite this, responsibility for customer care, service or satisfaction is often delegated (more accurately 'relegated') to a lower level of management, showing a distinct lack of appreciation of priorities, particularly for repeat business. If the customer is unsatisfied this can will not only rebound in terms of his own repeat purchases but will also have an effect in terms of others with whom he is in contact. The future of the business can only be assured by generating such repeat business and anything which imperils this, such as poor quality or lack of rapport in handling complaints, must be rectified. Such rectification is best achieved if the person responsible for the operation of the department or function operates at a senior level.

Complaint recourse

One advantage of ensuring a reporting route, even to the top level, is that should a customer care employee find themselves in a difficult situation with which they feel unable to cope, they can refer the awkward customer to a more senior person. Indeed, if the problem cannot be solved in (say) a five minute discussion or initial correspondence, a fresh negotiator may be essential to avoid irritation developing and positions polarising. Thus front line staff have senior support and will not feel that they are left to fend for themselves. If they continue some involvement at the more senior stage, they may also be able to benefit from seeing how the problem is handled at that more senior level.

It is doubtful if the initial contact at the company in case study 6.2 passed the matter upwards and no doubt the holidaymaker's personal letter to the Chairman was the first the latter knew of the problem. In sending for the file he would become aware of the previous correspondence which might not reflect well on those responsible. Indeed, those who try to snuff out such complaints should consider that, in the event of the complainant jumping managerial levels, their own incompetence may be exposed.

The black hole 83

Another advantage of placing responsibility for customer satisfaction at Board level is that it helps to avoid the 'black hole' of customer complaints. Where inadequate emphasis is put on the positive need to learn from complaints, and on the commitment to improving standards, there can be a perceived awareness that complaints reflect badly on the perpetrator and therefore the complaint must be either covered up or diverted at all costs.

Whilst the human motivation in such a situation may be understandable, it helps no-one:

- the customer gains nothing from having his complaint dismissed, indeed aggravation is the only effect.

- the company gains nothing. Almost certainly the customer will go elsewhere and may spread the word about his poor treatment, and

- the department or person responsible is left to continue perpetrating mistakes in the future.

Case study 7.1
Out in the open

It was company policy that although verbal complaints should try to be converted and satisfied at the sharp end of the business, whenever a written complaint was made it should be passed to the company secretary. The company's toy shops sold a considerable number of 'pocket money toys' – small value items which children could purchase themselves. Included in the range was a pair of scissors described as 'safety scissors' and designed to be suitable for a small child. A customer wrote to Head Office to complain that his young son had cut his mouth whilst playing with a pair of such scissors. The Secretary telephoned expressing his concern and suggesting he call in to see them.

'Hello, Mr Robinson, thank you for coming to see us, it is always nice to see our customers, even if it is a matter of complaint or query. Now what's the problem?'

'It's these scissors your Croydon shop are selling – my son has cut his mouth on them.'

'Oh I'm sorry to hear that – what's his name and how old is he?'

'Peter, and he was two, last week'

'Is it a bad cut – did it need stitches?'

'Well no, but it drew blood and he was upset for a couple of hours.'

'I hope he is better now ... (1) ... how did he get hold of the scissors?'

'They were one of his birthday presents we bought at your shop.'

'I would have thought two was a little young to be playing with scissors, surely children of that age tend to put everything in their mouths don't they, I know mine do?' (2)

'But the packaging states they are safety scissors so we thought it was safe' (3)

'Well of course the description "safety" refers to the fact that the blades themselves have no points and both blades, except the cutting edges, which are blunt of course, are covered in plastic. As I am sure you know, unlike knives, the blades of most scissors are actually fairly blunt.'

'How can scissors be blunt – they cut.'

'It is actually the scissor movement of the two blades which does the cutting. With these scissors, our manufacturers protect everything else but obviously cannot stop the scissor movement otherwise they would not be scissors at all. We call them safety scissors in the same way that the manufacturers of safety pins name their pins 'safety pins'. Safety pins are actually very much sharper than our scissors. That safety description refers to the fact that the sharp point of the pin is protected from the user – particularly small children and babies. Despite its name, the safety pin is sharp – indeed far sharper than any part of Peter's scissors. Obviously despite the protection that is part of the safety pin, you would never give one to your child to play with would you?' (3)

84

'But surely you should put on your packaging that they should not be given to young children.'

'We sell several thousand of these scissors each year and this is the first time we have heard of a cut. Obviously if there is anything we can do to avoid even a single recurrence we should examine it. I must say that we appreciate your coming here and telling us of this incident and hope that Peter has now fully recovered. What we would like to do is offer to reimburse your expenses for coming here and to give you this assortment of sweets which Peter definitely can put in his mouth, and we hope he enjoys them.' (5)

Key techniques

(1) As a result of a deliberate effort the tone of the conversation is friendly and the attitude is positive. The customer has been made welcome and concern has been expressed at the injury, although no indication of acceptance of liability has been given. Using the name of the child tries to personalise the conversation.

(2) Using a rhetorical question invites the father to agree with the statement, even though it contains an implied criticism of the family itself. Including a reference to the Secretary's own children tries to create a rapport regarding shared experiences and makes it clear that the ways of children and the need to protect them are known and appreciated first hand.

(3) This is awkward – the double-edged question. Accepting that the ages should be on the packaging could be taken as an admission of liability, whilst dismissing it would undermine the sense of a responsible and sensible retailer that is being sought. Care is needed in dealing with such questions/comments and here much of the real point is deliberately ignored.

(4) Using another rhetorical question gains some advantage, whilst the allegation that the scissors cannot be safe has been covered by the reference to a far more widely known product also used in connection with children. Such innovative thought is very valuable in these circumstances and demands pre-interview consideration.

(5) Without appearing too pushy, the Secretary seeks to conclude the interview. Mr Robinson had a complaint, but the company has a reasonable defence, offering reimbursement of expenses and a small gift should settle the matter. Obviously if it does not, then the company, mindful of the requirements of its Products Liability insurers may have to withdraw from further discussion and leave it to the insurers. Dealing with the matter by interview (rather than in writing) may actually benefit the company and its insurers as no written record remains.

In this instance the solution was achieved relatively smoothly mainly because the problem was handled by someone in a position of authority who was experienced enough to realise all the implications and to avoid all the pitfalls. Had this complaint been handled at a lower level in the company and/or without adequate briefing the outcome could have been potentially dangerous to the company's reputation. Imagine the effect on toy sales just before Christmas if Mr Robinson had been able to get national media coverage for his son's injury. Equally, in case study 6.2, the customer had access to national media and was prepared, in the absence of a suitable treatment and/or settlement, to make the dispute known to a TV holiday programme. If given prominence it could have caused considerable loss to the company's business.

The organisation ethos is that it wishes to learn from mistakes. This entails a commitment to learning from mistakes rather than conducting witch hunts. As long as this is the case then the propensity to cover up should be reduced. In his book *The triumph* John Galbraith comments 'a cardinal rule of American diplomacy is that one never dwells on the mistakes of another man...mistakes are inevitable. If they are not allowed to others, they will not be allowed to you.' The reciprocal nature of this attitude, similar to the adage that 'people in glass houses should not throw stones' is obvious. The attitude should be that whilst mistakes may be excused, provided the perpetrator learns from them and tries to avoid them in the future, a cover up of a mistake can never be countenanced. In this way positive commitment to complaint conversion and customer satisfaction can be engendered.

Case study 7.2
Stifling a response

The supplier had indicated a future change to both the telephone number and exchange of the subscriber. However although the company had stated the numbers would change it also stated that the actual change date would not be known with any degree of certainty until only a few weeks before the effective date. The subscriber rang the local office:

'Although you have indicated you will be making this change, you haven't given an effective date, which is absolutely crucial to us. We have an enormous number of changes to make to letterheads, adverts, notification to overseas contacts and so on, all of which will take time.'

'But we've already told you it is going to happen sometime in the early part of next year.'

'That's fine as far as it goes but it is nowhere near precise enough for us – we need to know an actual date well in advance. We have to book overseas advertising with our telephone number now. In addition, we have overseas customers as well as UK customers – who have to be told well in advance. If you feel unsure about completion, why not commit to a later date which gives plenty of leeway.'

'We have indicated an approximate date, we won't commit to a later date as we cannot afford to have equipment lying around idle – we need to get a good return for our shareholders.'

'Fine – but unless you satisfy your customers first, your shareholders will not be satisfied. As a customer who is also a shareholder I do not think either your attitude or your approach are correct.'

Key techniques

(1) The person forced to deal with this obviously had no idea of the real problem that an undated change of an essential lifeline for business would cause to a small business and adopted a dismissive attitude, the purpose of which was to try to snuff out the protest at an early stage. This might work with some customers, but the danger is that it will backfire, as it did here, thereby worsening the situation.

(2) Assuming that reference to the need to make a return on investment would silence the customer is patronising. The effect here was to irritate the customer/shareholder so much that recourse was made to the office of the Chairman of this large UK company. To the embarrassment of the local office the Chairman's office then became involved. Any possibility of snuffing out the problem not only failed but was a direct cause of the matter escalating into a much higher profile dispute.

The problem for the company in case study 7.2 was that it had previously introduced and distributed a document outlining in a high profile way its commitment to customer service and standards stating 'Our goal is for you, our customer to feel delighted with our service and the value for money we give to you'. Once the Chairman's office became involved, the local office quickly changed their attitude, agreed to give three month's notice of the change and thereafter kept the customer/shareholder fully informed at all stages of the work. This is a classic example of how trying to dismiss a problem and failing to grant respect to enquirers can backfire and create more serious problem encounters than originally existed .

Empowering the employees

The implementation by Reading Borough Council of the principle of empowering its receptionists so that they could decide whether members of the public should see council officials could not have been effected without training such staff to discover from the person requiring access what the problem was and who would be the most appropriate person to deal with it. This involves not only acquiring a considerable amount of information, names and areas of responsibilities, and so on, but also entails a clarification of the responsibilities of a variety of people within the organisation. Thus the adoption of a customer satisfaction, or complaints conversion programme may involve a large scale re-assessment of 'who does what' within the company.

Case study 7.3
A bouquet for London Transport

On the day I was commissioned to write this book, I had been giving a seminar in London and had not heard any travel news. On entering Covent Garden underground station, one of London Transport's staff shouted out to all those waiting for a lift to the platform that there were severe delays on the Piccadilly Line and we might do better to find an alternative route. Thanks to his action, prompted solely by consideration for his passengers, I used a different line and was saved considerable and frustrating delay.

Case study 7.4
A second bouquet for LT

The following morning I had to travel back into London. Access to the platform was barred by Inspectors making sure all passengers had a ticket before boarding a train. One passenger who, presumably, was used to jumping on a train without a ticket, missed a train because he had to queue for a ticket. As a result he was abusive to one of the Inspectors. The Inspector heard him out and then calmly pointed out that if he wished to take the matter further he should write to the Authorities who had instructed him to inspect all tickets at the station that morning.

> **Key technique**
> That is customer care at the sharp end from people who no doubt take more than their fair share of complaints. The whole system was having a number of problems at the time – not least being plagued by hoax bomb scares – and as a tangible representative no doubt the Inspector's ears had been bent by many of those whose journeys had been delayed. Delays were neither the fault of the representatives featured here nor was there anything they could do about them. Perhaps the passenger who missed his train felt better at having sounded off at someone who could not answer back in kind.

Bullying

In case study 7.4 the passenger was indulging himself in adopting a bullying attitude since he would know that ideally the Inspector could not respond to him in the same way that he had spoken. Inherent in dealing with complaints is a need to consider how to handle bullies. The tactic implicit in the actions of the bully is aggressiveness rather than assertiveness. The difference between the two is that the aggressive individual makes points and arguments very forcibly in a way that challenges or destroys the right of the target to respond. The bully assumes that no other views are feasible and consequently can be dismissed out of hand. If the subject of their bullying responds in like manner, it is often the case that they respond by trying to blame others. An assertive person can make the same points but without challenging the right of the respondent to reply, indeed accepting the right of the other party to hold differing views. The bully needs to realise that if we use aggression ourselves we may well generate aggression in return. Even if the subject needs to sublimate a response there may be other ways in which a response can be generated.

The best approach to the bully could be to:

■ let them explode or pressurise;

■ summarise their points, ignoring all emotive aspects and concentrating on the valid facts;

■ confront them with alternative facts and contentions without responding to the temper or pressure;

■ present an alternative in a way that enables them to save face.

Case study 7.5
Pointless aggression

The discussion between management and trade union had reached a delicate stage. A meeting was convened and a few minutes before the set time, the union representatives arrived at the office and, without stopping at reception, walked straight to the board room and occupied seats including that normally used by the Managing Director. When the MD arrived to commence the meeting he was infuriated by this total lack of manners and consequently refused all concessions then requested by the union.

Key technique

Whilst a demonstration of strength may assist – unnecessarily 'needling' an opponent achieves nothing other than possibly giving the instigator pleasure. Indeed such action may actually:
– create a backlash;
– harden the other party's views; and/or
– cause increased polarisation of the respective attitudes. Using this tactic is usually counter-productive as it moves neither party towards their desired result.

90

It should not be overlooked that a simple matter like taking a chair at a table at a meeting, particularly at a meeting called to try to reconcile a problem, makes a statement. The person that takes a chair at the head of the table, as did the union representative in case study 7.5 is indicating that he or she wishes to dominate the discussion. A customer taking such a chair is also indicating that he intends to dominate, that is be demanding during the discussion. His personality may tend to make him more of a leader or loner. Conversely, someone taking a seat along the side of a table flanked by other chairs is indicating that he wishes to be 'a team member' and thus may be expected to take a more reasonable and constructive attitude than the person at the head of the table. Knowing and understanding these differences, and thus making allowances for them in the way in which we then try to deal with the people concerned may provide us with a valuable perception of their motivation.

8

Doasyouwouldbedoneby

Key learning points

1 Avoiding assumptions, jumping to conclusions and instant solutions is essential. Complaints need objective and individual consideration.

2 The person who can perceive a customer's real views and attitudes has more chance of being able to succeed in dealing.

3 Facts are needed before any decision is made, and everything needs to be kept simple, clear and unambiguous.

4 We need to treat customers as we would wish to be treated were we in the same situation.

Getting the facts

As already noted, often the main problem in dealing or attempting to deal with demanding customers is that we may have an imprecise view of the problem itself or try to solve it before we have fully understood either the problem or our opponent fully. Oriental civilisations generally take more time to consider matters than we do in the West. They will consider items from a number of angles, often using several teams to consider the same problem. Each team discusses alternative approaches before liaising to discuss the alternatives. Only then do they commit themselves to a chosen route. They also tend to devote considerable time and effort to studying their opponent, assessing strengths and weaknesses, looking for leverage and opportunities to exploit. Conversely, in the West, we often tend to confuse activity with productivity and because of this sometimes find ourselves under pressure to act without having considered fully all the implications. In responding to such pressure with action, we may be forced to:

- make assumptions;

- jump to conclusions; and

- provide instant solutions which can either be inappropriate or create a further problem.

Diagnosis

'Assume' tends to make an 'ass' of 'u' and 'me'. If we try to reach a conclusion based on an assumption, we may end up with no meeting of minds. In trying to provide an instant solution, any lack of perception of the true cause of the problem and/or the desired effect of the other party will ensure failure. Far better to investigate, to discover all the facts **before** attempting to form a conclusion. A corollary here may be the procedure adopted by an experienced doctor, who usually asks a number of questions concerning symptoms and causes, to try to establish a resumé of all the facts before reaching a diagnosis. We would do well to emulate this diagnostic approach when dealing with demanding customers, as without the facts we can be trapped into making assumptions.

Case study 8.1
A fishy story

The customer was a small business dependent upon personal contact with a number of clients. As an appreciation of the clients' business, he ordered a number of Christmas gifts, principally sides of smoked salmon. Partly as a check, he also included an order for himself. Since by 22nd December he had not received his order he checked with a number of his clients and found to his dismay that they too had received nothing. He rang the gift company and was told:

- *'The trouble with late orders is that there is a danger that we cannot source the items quickly enough to meet the Christmas rush.'* (1)

- *'We are sure that they are all on their way and if not received by Christmas they will be immediately afterwards.'* (2)

- *'There is nothing we can do in any case as we are closing down now'.* (3)

> **Key techniques**
> (1) The assumption made by the company, as it had received a large number of late orders, was that this customer's order was one of those. In fact, the order had not only been placed well before the date advertised as 'last orders' but had even been acknowledged by the company before that date.
> (2) How could the company make this assumption without checking and further, how could it assume that if the goods were received after Christmas that would be satisfactory?
> (3) No comment is necessary. The customer, in seeking recompense after the holiday, was scathing about their total lack of respect for their customers, pointing out that the whole of the continuation of their business rested on their ability to satisfy those who had placed orders for pre-Christmas delivery and to make arrangements for suitable customer service should things go wrong. In fact, so conclusive was the proof of their poor service that the company replaced the whole order – some fortunate clients thus receiving two gifts!

93

Apart from the poor customer service and respect evinced by the company, its overriding fault was that of making assumptions, which were entirely unfounded. No time was spent ascertaining or checking the facts. This is a shaky basis from which to try and negotiate any settlement and may hand an edge to the other side. After all, if one statement can be shown to be false, the reliability of all other statements then becomes questionable.

Jumping to conclusions

Whilst making assumptions is based on a lack of knowledge or understanding of the facts, jumping to conclusions tends to be generated by an imperfect knowledge of the facts. Although some facts may be known, coming to conclusions based only upon them, without checking or corroboration can be equally dangerous.

Case study 8.2
A second fishy story

Despite the customer proving the facts of the case to the Christmas food gift company, things did not improve as expected. The replacement smoked salmon for the customer himself failed to be delivered and another argument developed. During this repeat performance, it seemed to the customer that the company had concluded that he was trying to defraud them and they had decided to resist. Having had to threaten them with legal action, they eventually agreed to send yet another salmon which arrived by virtually the same post as the original replacement. Since the original replacement was in a less than fresh state, the parties had to assume (the only time in the encounter when an assumption was probably justified), that it had been delayed in the post. At least it proved to the company that the customer's comments had been valid.

Postscript: Since this type of business is susceptible to theft, one can sympathise with the attitude of the company. However, one cannot assume that, if some are 'trying it on', that therefore **all** customers are doing so. Such an attitude merely aggravates.

94
Instant solutions

Whilst it is vital to deal with problems and demands courteously and swiftly, to minimise aggravation, care needs to be taken that responses are not made which have the effect of 'closing down the encounter'. This may solve the initial problem but only at the expense of creating another, when the attitude may be aggravated.

Case study 8.3
Non-delivery

The newspaper delivery service was erratic. One morning the customer's paper was not delivered and he went round to the shop.
'I can't understand that – and we have no spares here.'
'Fine – so I am without a paper for the fourth time in two weeks.'
'Tell you what, I've got to go out later I will get you one and deliver it myself.'
'Right.'
Perhaps needless to say no later delivery transpired. The following day:
'What happened to the paper you were going to get and deliver for me?'
'I didn't go out, so I didn't get it.'
'You had promised to deliver it to me yesterday afternoon.'
'But I didn't have one.'

'No, and now you no longer have a contract to deliver my papers and I do not expect a charge for delivery to be levied for the last two weeks in view of the poor service.'

Key technique
The instant solution seemed to settle a problem but this would only have been possible if the promise given had been kept, in which case, customer relations would have been improved. As it was, a failure to live up to the promised instant solution did not put the two parties back where they were, it aggravated the whole situation.

Perception

If assumptions, swift conclusions and instant solutions are to be out-lawed, the question then remains to be answered 'How then should we proceed?' The simple secret is that we must have a good perception or understanding of people, which is easy to say and sadly not so easy to achieve. Yet in attempting to move customers to a desired result, their views and opinions, prejudices and preferences, attitudes and previous reactions must all be taken into account to guide us towards an under-standing of what they want. If this sounds somewhat political, that is hardly surprising, as, after all, politics has been defined as the art of the possible, and what is being suggested is that if we have determined a particular outcome we need to consider how to convert others to our way of thinking.

An old saying runs 'The reason we have one mouth and two ears is so that we can listen twice as much as we talk'. Sadly in practice this tends to be the exception, and is aggravated by the passive state of hearing being mistaken for the active state of actually listening to what a person is saying. Indeed active listening requires us to consider not only what a person says, but also what they do not say, and what can be inferred from body language, attitudes and actions. After all, a person is quite capable of a multiple response to a given situation. He may well reply to the same question in totally different terms to his boss, his colleagues, his subordinate, his peers or mates and his wife, whilst all the time keeping his real feelings strictly to himself! Human beings are complex characters quite capable of having at least the sev-eral different views just identified, and, further of varying such views depending solely upon the interface of the moment. Perception is an art by which we try to understand not just what is said, but what the other party may wish to say, as well as their real feelings.

Conditioning the opposition

The ability to perceive the other party's real viewpoint and to visualise how the problem and suggestions will be viewed through their eyes can be a valuable tactic in the respondent's approach to a complaint discussion. Recognising what the other party really seeks enables you to consider providing it, or at least to consider the implications of providing it. Those responsible for dealing with customer complaints initially could follow a procedure like that set out in Figure 8.1.

1 Ensure all complaints/comments/observations are recorded in a register with date.

2 Ensure some action is taken within, say, 48 hours, even if this is only an acknowledgment.

3 Research and uncover the facts, customer, order, payment record.

4 Listen carefully to the complaint, noting all relevant information.

5 Check any facts put forward or disputed by the customer.

6 Try to identify what the customer wants or needs as their desired aim. Consider whether it is possible to offer what is required.

7 Be courteous, tactful and pleasant at all times. Never raise your voice, allow irritation or anger to show, or be in any way patronising, insulting or sarcastic.

8 Only if the complaint is straightforward, venture to attempt a solution and even then only after consideration of both the apparent and underlying implications.

9 If it is not possible to provide the customer's ideal solution, consider whether some compromise might be acceptable, and, if so try to introduce the idea into the conversation.

10 In more complicated cases, thank the customer for bringing the matter to the organisation's attention, apologise for any inconvenience and state that the matter will be investigated rigorously.

11 Set a time limit by which the customer will receive an answer or further contact, and ensure that time limit is maintained.

12 Investigate the complaint and consider the validity of the customer's

case objectively. Derive a possible response with a fall back position if the customer refuses to accept the first suggestion.

13 Consider any precedent that might be created by a settlement and weigh that up against any potential backlash from publicity. Although it is often said that there is no such thing as bad publicity, this cannot be true where poor or faulty products can be exposed, or the safety of the consumer put at risk.

14 Try to conclude the dispute harmoniously, with the aim of enhancing the reputation of the company.

Figure 8.1 Customer satisfaction guidelines

Doasyouwouldbedoneby

Often demanding encounters are caused as much by entrenched atti-tudes or misconceptions as by the original fault. 'Dealers' need to keep an open mind, to avoid starting the encounter with any prejudices, or preconceptions. In this way the discussion can at least commence with some degree of clarity. However 'dealers' also need to try to use their perception or understanding to put themselves in the customer's place and see things through their eyes in order to understand **their** atti-tude. In *The Water Babies*, Charles Kingsley refers to the 'loveliest fairy in the world and her name is Mrs. Doasyouwouldbedoneby'. If we treat others as we would wish to be treated, were we in the same position ourselves, then almost certainly our comprehension of the other party's viewpoint will be considerable, and we will improve the chances of our being able to conclude the encounter in a positive, and mutually satis-factory, manner. For this reason we need to ensure that those respond-ing and those complaining have similar outlooks on the problem.

Case study 8.4
Insensitive – and inappropriate

In a very poor and run down inner city area was an advertisement hoard-ing showing a beautiful country cottage. The advertisement was promot-ing the advantages of saving with a particular building society and bore a slogan the inference of which was that if one saved with this society such a retirement location could be the depositors' for the asking. Across the bottom of the hoarding someone, using a spray can, had added the leg-end 'we should be so lucky'. It was exceedingly difficult, if not impossible to imagine that many of the deprived inhabitants of such a run down area could be projected into such an attractive and expensive location. In short the advertisement was out of touch with its target audience in that area.

In seeking to deal with problems, those responsible need to be able to relate to and understand the customer. There is little point in someone who lives in a mansion on a 100 acre estate supported by a personal staff of maids and gardeners, trying to field the problems experienced by tenants living in a run down inner city tower block. Their comprehension of the problems is most unlikely to be anywhere near the reality under consideration. If someone from such a background did try to deal with problems, not only is a solution unlikely, the customers may feel they are being patronised which could add insult to injury. Similarly it will be difficult for someone from a very low income background to try to deal with queries and problems being raised by customers at the other end of the social scale. The inevitable misunderstandings and lack of comprehension may provide suitable material for amusing television situation comedies but are not amusing in real life. Thus the receptionist in the garage who lacks comprehension of the problems associated with vehicle servicing and repair, and the inconvenience caused during the loss of the vehicle for such work, is likely to irritate rather than help customers. This will also be the result if the doctor's receptionist sees the job as protecting the doctor from the patients rather than the means for finding the best way for the doctor to serve as many patients as possible. Both these examples illustrate instances where the attitudes evinced can actually create demanding customers.

Empathy

What was missing from the society sponsoring the advertisement in case study 8.3 and from the examples cited immediately above was any empathy with the target audience. The dictionary defines 'empathy' as 'the power of projecting one's personality into (and so fully comprehending) the object', the operative word being 'so', since it is the act of projection that allows us to comprehend the other side's views more completely. If respondents to demanding customers have empathy with those making such demands then greater understanding will result and conflict can be averted in many cases. Perception, empathy and a 'doasyouwouldbedoneby' attitude, plus attention to the practical techniques outlined here, create a formidable combination in the armoury of problem encounter negotiators and are, sad to say, all too seldom found in those who have to deal with such problems. In addition, the therapeutic and often very effective, device of simply listening to another's problems, the approach adopted by caring organisations such as the Samaritans, can be equally effective. If someone takes the trouble to listen to and make a note of the complaint, that alone, without any further action, may actually be sufficient to 'draw the sting' of the complaint. Then without any corrective action, a problem can be reduced from the original burning issue to a mere minor irritation. Conversely, a refusal to accept the terms of the complaint at all will merely serve to inflame what may already be a contentious issue.

Case study 8.5
Listening improves quality

There had been a number of complaints regarding the quality and choice of the food available in the staff restaurant over a number of years. The newly appointed Personnel Manager became aware of these and invited two of the chief protagonists of the complaints to come and see her to discuss the matter.

'I understand you are very concerned about the restaurant.'

'You bet we are – we've been on about the quality and poor choice for ages but no-one seems to take any notice and nothing gets done.'

'I see, well as you know I'm new, so if you can bear repeating all the problems I will certainly consider them and see if we can meet at least some of your complaints. I must first say that I am very concerned about the restaurant since its finances are in my budget and we do not seem to be getting value for the money we are investing.'

The complaining employees outlined the main causes of their concern during a fairly long meeting, and in turn the Personnel Manager set out the problems the company was experiencing with the financing. It was agreed that a Catering Committee should be set up to consider ways and means of improving the situation. Before it convened for the first time and before any action had been taken regarding the complaints, one of the complainants sought the Personnel Manager to thank her for the improvements that had already been put into operation.

> **Key technique**
> Listening constructively, and to some degree sympathetically, to complaints rather than dismissing them out of hand created a situation where it seemed to the employees that improvements had already been put in hand! Subsequently considerable improvements were made and a regular process of price increases was introduced to bring the subsidy back under control. Even though this raised the costs to the employees, because the initiative had been seized and those affected were involved, the 'reduce the subsidy' policy was accepted without problem. The fact that improvements were also introduced as promised helped acceptance.

Exercising discretion

100

Obviously in trying to reconcile differences and settle opposing claims, some degree of negotiation will be essential (see Chapter 9). However, in taking the initiatives of studying the customer, understanding their motives and preferences, trying to relate to them and their preferences and endeavouring to satisfy them, we will already go a long way towards reaching a solution. Discretion within pre-set limits needs to be granted to those dealing with complaints so that minor items can be settled swiftly.

In case study 4.1 the amounts in question were small – only £4 for the oversupply and £50 for the unauthorised overprinting cost. Had the first company representative to deal with the problem suggested an immediate credit of, say, £15 for both the oversupply and the fact that the order was late, the dispute over £50 might never have arisen, and neither would the company have needed to spend so much time trying to resolve a dispute which rapidly snowballed in complexity and scope. Conversely, a junior or untrained member of staff initially handling a situation should not be left unsupported in that position should the dispute develop into a more difficult situation. This applies whether the organisation is responding to or initiating the negotiation.

Simplicity

We should not overlook the necessity of keeping everything as straightforward as possible. The guidelines here are to:

- keep it simple;
- make it clear;
- avoid ambiguity and at all times to;
- recognise the interests of the consumer;

in order to generate comprehension, cohesion and commitment.

Keep it simple

When getting the facts and putting over other facts for consideration, attention to simplicity in order to try to ensure the minimum incidence of misunderstanding is essential. This may involve some repetition to ensure that comprehension has been achieved. In dealing with the communication problems that tend to be the root cause of many problem encounters, such communication should be kept simple, uncluttered and clear. Although this should be obvious, all too often the aim can be foiled by the use of unclear and complex messages which confuse rather than enlighten, and hamper, rather than help solve, problems.

101

Make it clear

Messages tend to become confused if they are passed through a number of intermediaries, the classic example being the oft-quoted change of the field officer's message 'Send reinforcements we're going to advance' to the Headquarter's signal officer's received message of 'Send three and fourpence we're going to a dance'. After all, if only 10 per cent of a message is lost each time it is relayed by one person to another, over 50 per cent of the original import can be lost between the executive Board's original request and its receipt by the shop floor employee, if it has to pass through the average organisation's five layers. The utmost clarity of instruction and comprehension of the situation and clear limits of their discretion should be engendered to problem 'dealers'.

Avoid ambiguity

This involves using simple everyday English and avoiding jargon. Jargon has been called the 'refuge of the lazy and the protection of the insecure'. Those who are lazy tend to use jargon as a short cut rather than translating it into normal English, whilst those who are insecure tend to use it to protect their position: the hidden message being conveyed is 'since you do not understand the jargon, you are not one of us in the clique'. Alternatively we can get trapped into a situation where we use jargon forgetting that others may not understand. Not only will the words not be understood but also they can become an irritant **because** the other party is baffled. Jargon thus becomes a bar to effective communication which is the key to the solution of all problem encounters.

Case study 8.6
Getting it right

SPAR Foodliner is a supermarket in the village of Treherbert in the Rhondda Valley which has invested a considerable amount of time in endeavouring to reduce the time a customer has to wait at a checkout to pay for the goods selected. If queues start to build then staff are immediately switched from other work to manning the tills. This has enabled the outlet to reduce waiting times to, it claims, two and a half to three minutes average and five minutes maximum, which is much shorter than many of the supermarket's big rivals.

This resembles the commitment of Lloyds Bank, as featured in one of their television advertisements to open more cashiers positions if there are people waiting, thereby demonstrating a real commitment to, and respect for, their customers.

These commitments to giving good service and thus reducing customer annoyance and the incidence of complaints can be contrasted with the attitude of some organisations who on telephoning with a complaint (or even an order) place you in a call-stacking arrangement and play music to you. Waiting and listening for more than 20 seconds should be impossible but does happen – or alternatively during the movement of the stack, you are cut off and in order to make your, by then aggravated, protest you need to redial only to find you are back in the queue again.

> **Key technique**
> The real interests of the consumer need to take priority and using technology may have attractions but no real advantages. Companies who operate these telephone stacking systems tend to exude a compla-

cent attitude that stacking customers' calls solves all ills. It tends not to – and indeed can aggravate those customers left waiting, particularly as they are normally paying for the delay. If companies have that number of calls what is needed is not a stacking system but more lines and more operators and a real commitment to customer service.

Postscript:
Care needs to be taken in choosing music to be used by such stacking systems. An incautious choice can create unintended amusement and unwanted effects. On telephoning one company investigating overcharging, I was bemused to find myself listening to the theme from 'The Sting' – a film about confidence tricksters. A somewhat unfortunate choice.

Whilst problems are caused with telephone stacking, there are a number of organisations which operate solely by telephone which seem able to get it right. Writing in the *Sunday Times* in December 1993, Diana Wright, the Personal Finance editor, referred to a reader's letter praising the excellent service given by one of the largest telephone banking operations, and commented that she had heard nothing but good about the operation. So it is possible to get it right – and to gain public recognition for the endeavour. Research carried out by First Direct (the telephone banking system referred to) indicates that 94 per cent of its customers believe its service to be superior to that of traditional banks and a third of its customers join because of personal recommendations.

Presumably the secret is that if you set up something from scratch you give attention to all the ramifications and seek to get it right first time. Thus First Direct requires its personnel to complete an eight week induction programme before anyone is allowed to take their first call. The bank recognises that the voice on the end of the phone must sound positive and customer friendly and works towards this end.

Getting it right when welding such a system on to an existing set-up seems a far more difficult operation, or perhaps it is just that short cuts are taken and assumptions made. It certainly seems very odd that organisations that have evolved a system requiring their staff to deal with customers over the telephone do not seem to be able to get the procedure operating as efficiently and effectively as newcomers such as First Direct. Perhaps what is lacking is care for the customer – the same care that prompts First Direct to use an 0345 telephone number so that no matter from where in the country a customer calls, they are only charged at local call rate.

103

9

Negotiation

> **Key learning points**
>
> 1 Research the other party before attempting negotiation.
>
> 2 Determine tactics likely to enable you to achieve your desired result.
>
> 3 Consider whether you can adopt a fall-back position if the preferred outcome cannot be achieved.
>
> 4 The use of Alternative Disputes resolution can save time and money.

Research

Demanding customer 'dealers' need to have experience in and command of negotiation skills and tactics in attempting to achieve consensus. In conflict, since the preferences of both parties may be impossible to achieve, solutions may have to be presented on a 'sliding scale', from the ideal, through acceptable compromises to an unacceptable, and therefore confrontational position. Having identified the other party's preferences, views and prejudices and having made attempts to empathise with them and considered reversing positions to try to understand their point of view, we also need to try and discover as much as possible about them in order to assess their likely preferred and fall-back positions. This may require a certain amount of research but such preparation may be well-rewarded, as long as it provides accurate data.

Case study 9.1
Unfortunate briefing

At the Group of Seven summit meeting in Tokyo in July 1993, the USA provided guidance information for its delegates. Unfortunately their research was somewhat faulty:

– the Italian president, who has no executive power and does not attend such meetings, was shown as leading the delegation, whereas the Italian prime minister, who has such power and leads Italy's delegation to the meetings, was not listed.

– details of the other two main members of the Italian delegation, the treasury and foreign ministers, were also omitted but details of the finance minister, who was not due to and did not attend the meeting, were included.

> **Key technique**
> If information is produced to assist negotiations, no matter what the arena, it must be accurate. If not it may be preferable to forget the idea, as faulty information can lose respect, create communication bars and may even be insulting, albeit unwittingly, thus resulting in the creation of the opposite effect to that intended or required.

105

Negotiation

Discussing problems and complaints requires negotiation skills and entails the use of certain principles and practices as listed in Figure 9.1.

> 1 Establish the facts in order to arrive at an initial view.
> 2 Try to anticipate what the other party's view will be.
> 3 Accept that there are two sides to every story and that the other party may hold different views even for apparently illogical reasons.
> 4 Research the background of the other party and endeavour to assess their manner of approach.
> 5 Give weight and credence to the views of the other side. Dismissing such views out of hand is likely to provoke a negative backlash. Well-founded flattery, used with discretion, can be very compelling.
> 6 Sublimate your own prime preferences to achieve consensus and assess whether there is a substitutional solution acceptable to both. Such 'British compromises' at least have the advantage of allowing things to progress.
> 7 Try to make constant movements towards the desired result, ensuring that a flexible approach is adopted and that an entrenched position does not close off possible progress towards the ideal or substitutional end.
> 8 Be ready to compromise, it may not be ideal but at least it may enable progress to continue.

Figure 9.1 Negotiation principles

Tactics

A number of tactics can be employed in order to try to ensure one's preferred outcome prevails such as are set out in the checklist in Figure 9.2.

```
 1 Finding the edge
 2 Non-disclosure
 3 Misinformation
 4 Face-saving
 5 Pressure
 6 Threats
 7 Letting the other party make the running
 8 Silence
 9 Punching cotton wool
10 Rubbing salt in the wound
11 Fishing
12 Misunderstanding
13 Temper
14 Sympathy
15 Under-estimating
16 Layering (the sliding scale of preferences)
17 Divide and rule
18 Pre-emption
```

Figure 9.2 Summary of negotiation tactics

Finding the edge

This involves attempting to discover if there is any pressure which can be brought to bear on the other party to agree to the solution preferred by the company.

Case study 9.2
Applying an edge

X in Essex and Y in Birmingham were engaged in negotiations usually conducted by post. However, Y suggested that they meet in London as he was prepared to travel and could arrange 'other business' which he could deal with at the same time. X agreed to the meeting but with an apparently considerable reluctance. However, what he knew but Y did not know that he knew, was that Y had a girl friend in London and wanted any excuse to get to that city, particularly if his company would pay the costs of him getting there. X then used his apparent reluctance as a lever to exert extra concessions from Y as a *quid pro quo* for re-arranging his diary to oblige Y with the London-based meeting.

Key technique
Gaining as much information about the other party and their situation and case is essential. Information is power.

Non-disclosure

The principle here is to start the discussion without using all the relevant facts. If satisfactory progress towards the object of the encounter is not made, the use of such facts at a later stage may help the instigator to carry the day. Not using all one's 'ammunition' at the first onslaught does enable a fresh attack to be mounted later. Having said that, sometimes it can be preferable to overwhelm the opposition by means of a pre-emptive move.

Case study 9.3
Holding back

J and K were conducting a rent review discussion. K, as the Landlord's agent was, trying to gain the best rent possible and had put forward a number of examples of rents of other nearby shops, some of which J, representing the tenant, knew to be a distortion of the reality. J commenced arguing the case on the basis of the evidence provided by K as if he accepted it at face value. By prolonging the negotiations and using the delay for additional research, J became aware of the full facts concerning the hidden deals he already knew about. However he did not use this information until K had already given way to some extent from his first position. When J then introduced this additional evidence, K had to further reduce his demand.

> **Key technique**
> Using two or more items of information separately may contrive advantages greater than using them together; after all, one never knows, until it is too late, when the same tactic may be employed by the other party!

Misinformation

This involves indicating a far worse situation initially than is the case and then backtracking. Research shows that where this is utilised the hidden (and real) 'alternative' will gain acceptance in around 66 per cent of instances.

Case study 9.4
The acceptable price rise

The manufacturer wished to increase the price of his goods to the customer who would have considerable difficulty sourcing the products elsewhere. He invited the customer to lunch, thus gaining an edge by playing host, and indicated that prices would have to rise by 10 per cent. During the courses, as the customer argued vehemently against the suggestion, he continued to put forward all the facts and evidence supporting the increase. However as coffee arrived the manufacturer suggested a compromise 5 per cent increase, which is what he expected in the first place. The customer, relieved that he had avoided a 10 per cent increase, and believing that his vehemence in opposing the suggestion had paid off, agreed.

Face-saving

Allowing the other party to save 'face', particularly if the meeting takes place within an high-profile scenario, or on behalf of others, for example negotiating on behalf of trades union members, can be very effective. Since consensus is the desired result, the instigator needs to design the conduct of the meeting to make it appear that both sides have gained something, regardless of the facts.

Case study 9.5
The 10p face-saver

The predator made what was intended to be a pre-emptive takeover bid at a price well above the market price. The defending board refused to recommend the bid and shareholders were left to make up their own mind without guidance. The bid was eventually successful and the predator's chairman remonstrated with one of the defending directors. 'Why didn't you recommend our bid – you knew it was a good price?' 'But you left us nothing to do.' came the reply. 'If you had bid slightly lower, and then we talked, we could have given a recommendation at the price at which you bid. We would have been seen to have done something for our shareholders which would have saved face.'

Pressure

Pressure may need to be applied in some encounters in order to achieve progress, particularly where there are differences of opinion, which seem to be impossible to reconcile. Latent pressure may consist of a swift resumé of arguments, perhaps indicating the apparent weakness of the other's case with the aim of gaining agreement, whereas actual pressure attempts to force the issue.

Case study 9.6
Applying pressure

Case study 11.1 relates the circumstances of a high profile and public dispute. During that dispute the customer declared he was a shareholder and also was prepared to take the matter to the local Trading Standards officer. One can only guess whether the store's capitulation was prompted by this application of pressure, but it certainly indicated that the customer took the matter very seriously and had means to apply further pressure.

Threats

Although perhaps indicating a party's resolve, a threat can only be issued once, and the adage 'never issue a threat unless you are prepared to carry it out' should not be overlooked. Indeed, since the prime purpose of negotiation is to try to achieve consensus, threats should not really form part of such debate.

Case study 9.7
Bluff calling

The agency dealt with private individuals many of whom liked to try to obtain a concession or refund or 'allow a discount next time around' if there was a problem. The agency's difficulty was that many of the clients knew each other and rewarding a 'hard case' in this way could create a costly precedent. Accordingly it redesigned its paperwork and in future when clients registered, they were requested to ' ... read our terms and only if you are happy with them sign and return the registration form'. A problem subsequently arose with a client who demanded a refund for non-performance of a temporary staff contract.

110

'I must insist you refund my fee or I will report you.' she stated as her opening remark.

The agency tactfully tried to discover what had happened and having obtained the facts, pointed out that she was out of guarantee and therefore not entitled to any refund.

'I've never read that. If you don't give me my fee back I'm getting straight on to the Department of Employment.' shouted the client.

'I am sorry Mrs Robinson,' came the reply *'although of course you are perfectly entitled to contact the Department of Employment, since they have a copy of our terms, they will tell you as I am doing now that you are out of guarantee and there is no refund. Those are our terms which you accepted.'*

'But I've never accepted that.' she retorted almost incoherently. The agency pointed out that they held her registration form with her signature under a confirmation that said she had read, understood and agreed to such terms.

Key technique

Having shown the client that it had no liability, the agency could back away without further commitment, or alternatively might gain goodwill by granting a discount on a repeat order. Had its procedure and terms not supported its position no such flexibility would exist – underlining once again the essential need to get the terms right.

Letting the other side make the running

The principle here is to allow the other party to put forward their whole case, even including any extra data they were hoping to hold back, before putting forward any arguments or facts oneself. This is one of the principles of interrogation: 'Let them say what they want and lead them on'. In other words whilst someone is speaking he reveals more and more of his case and preferences, allowing the other party to conserve his ammunition for later. This can be alternatively described as 'keeping one's powder dry'.

Case study 9.8
Jumped too quickly

The two sides had been in dispute for some time. Eventually the company decided that it would give way to a limited extent to gain agreement with its supplier. Accordingly the director requested a meeting with his opposite number. Since the meeting had been requested at their initiative, one would presume that they had something new to offer. However, virtually as soon as they met, the supplier offered to settle at the director's latest figure. Had the supplier waited to see why the company had requested the meeting they would have found the company had moved towards them, rather than *vice versa*.

111

Silence

When Sir Thomas More was facing imprisonment and execution for refusing to acknowledge Henry VIII as head of the church in England he agreed to keep silent on the topic. However the very fact of his silence, in Henry's view, 'screamed up and down throughout Europe'. Silence can indicate a number of attitudes and many people cannot cope with it. Such people feel a pressure to fill the vacuum by speaking. In speaking, more of their case is revealed, whilst the quiet party gains ammunition for any counter-play. Silence is a particularly effective weapon in a two party face-to-face encounter but it needs strong nerves to stick with it.

Case study 9.9
Steeling one's nerves with silence

The two agents had agreed to meet having corresponded for some months to try to agree terms for a new lease. C, the landlord's agent, had initially been very bullish, suggesting a high rent but with the remainder of the terms as before. D's arguments on behalf of the tenant had worn him down somewhat and at the meeting, after a re-examination of evidence and counter-evidence a compromise rent was agreed.

C then tried to raise the question of original terms in the new lease, at which point D stated that the negotiations had all been on the basis of 'as existing apart from the rent' and that he did not see what more there was to be said. D continued that the rent had been negotiated and agreed on that basis and that seemed to conclude the discussion. He then kept quiet. C reviewed the situation to where it then rested. D did not reply. C pointed out that the lease was in an old form. D did not reply.

Key technique
By not replying D put pressure on C, and in the absence of counter-arguments C could only go over old ground again and again – he had nothing left to say.

Punching cotton wool

This can be a valuable response particularly where the other party is seized by temper. In answer to a particularly annoyed or outraged other party, if the first party keeps quiet, ultimately the second party will run out of original things to say, will need to keep repeating themselves and may ultimately dry up. Certainly 'dealers' need to allow someone seized by temper to have the whole of their say before trying to progress matters. Interrupting or correcting statements during a tirade is likely only to inflame.

Case study 9.10
I'm a fan but ...

The fan of the actress was incensed at some apparent slight. He bounded into her dressing room and delivered a long harangue, at the end of which she replied quietly 'And?' He repeated much of what he had said before and as his speech petered out she repeated 'And?' But by then he had had enough and rushed from the room. Because she refused to be drawn into a discussion of the item, he could not think of anything more to say. He had expected a defence or counter-attack but when none came was left with nothing fresh to attack.

Rubbing salt in the wound

This tactic entails repeated reference to the previous activity of the other side. Most people, if they lose out in a negotiation, try to ignore the defeat, applying a balm of silence to wounded pride. However, it may be possible to use the fact that the other side gained the upper hand previously as a lever in the current negotiations. Obviously this would only be of use should the negotiations be a repeat of a previous encounter.

113

Case study 9.11
The biter bit

In negotiations over a contract with their American supplier, the UK distributor had been unfairly treated by the other side, and forced to conclude a deal whereby they paid 10 per cent more for goods of a slightly inferior quality. At the following negotiations, rather than ignoring what had gone before, this fact was referred to repeatedly, until the supplier caved in and accepted that the previous negotiations had been too one-sided and agreed a deal beneficial to the distributor as part compensation and part apology for the previous tough deal.

Fishing

Keeping quiet forces other parties to speak whereas 'fishing' involves making extreme statements to generate response to keep the other party talking. Again the purpose is to encourage him to disclose more and more of his case and show how deeply he is committed to it.

Case study 9.12
A slip of the tongue

The landlords were being very bullish about the rent they were demanding at the review and had quoted a new letting they had concluded nearby which supported the rent they quoted. The director had spoken to the tenants of the other unit but had not been able to gain much information. When he came to negotiate with the landlords he pointed out that they could not substantiate the rent they demanded as their figure ignored the effect of the capital sum they had paid the new tenants to take the lease and the fact that they had waived the tenant paying their legal costs. 'How did you know about that?' was the landlord's agents instinctive retort.

> **Key technique**
> The director's fishing bluff had worked and without any details he managed to reduce the rental asking price.

Misunderstanding

114

By deliberately misinterpreting the other's comments and statements, the depth of feeling on a particular subject can be revealed. This can also be used in a meeting as a ploy to ruffle the presentation of the person putting forward a case. Conversely, if it is being used against you, you need to be aware of the device and to patiently explain the point again. Indeed it can be turned against the perpetrator with words such as 'I am sorry you don't understand, I thought I had made it fairly clear but I'll just run through the points again.' If the instigator's aim was to put you off your stroke and draw the encounter to a swift closure, calmly running through the arguments again will be the last thing he wants as it implies inattention on his part, and to some extent hands you an edge.

Temper

Deliberate loss of temper during an encounter in order to try to impress the other party how seriously the subject matter is being taken can be effective and act as an indication of commitment, however it can hardly be re-used in the same forum and, for this reason, should be used with extreme caution.

Case study 9.13
Temper wins the day

The meeting had been called to discuss the implementation of a promised resignation by a director once certain events had been put in place. The director prevaricated by indicating that his resignation would now take effect only after the calling of a shareholders' meeting. At this the acting chairman exploded in part real and part sham temper, pointing out in no uncertain terms, that this was a real life situation, the company was in serious danger of failing and no-one wishing to save it had time to split hairs concerning the manner of a resignation essential to clear the way for a capital re-structuring. Such was the vehemence of the reaction from a normally quietly spoken and reserved man, that it was generally agreed to have played a major part in achieving the director's resignation without further ado.

> **Key technique**
> Such deliberate loss of temper may be an effective ploy in certain circumstances although in encounters with customers it is unlikely to be appropriate.

115

Sympathy and under-estimation

Trying to engender sympathy for one's present position or problems may engender some rapport but, since it tends to give an impression of weakness, it is unlikely to be successful. Thus in case study 4.3 the advertising representative tried to generate sympathy from the client by inferring that she was so poorly paid that she was not inclined to devote time to the problem now confronting her. It was hardly surprising that the agency ignored the comment, after all, her personal terms relating to her employment were a matter solely for agreement between her and her employer. Creating in the mind of one's opponent an impression of your own apparent failings, that is an underestimation of ability, may work since it may relax their attitude possibly allowing you to slip arguments through. The danger is that having created the underestimation it can be difficult to gain a true estimation and appropriate credence for one's views. Underestimating one's opponent of course is a classic mistake, often causing greater disclosure of the case, believing success to be a foregone conclusion.

Layering

Whilst using the techniques described above may help move the encounter forward, inevitably some encounters will end in stalemate with no party willing to budge. Obviously there will need to be some compromise or settlement at some stage. Recognising the reality of the situation, negotiators need to layer their position with a sliding scale of preferences. Thus if their ideal outcome is not feasible, is there an alternative, not ideal but one with which they can live. It may be that there are two or three such alternatives which gradually move towards the other's position. Eventually there must come a point beyond which movement cannot be made. This also needs to be realised and accepted. Inevitably in moving down the scale of layers towards the final sticking point, one would anticipate corresponding movement by the other party, eventually leading to a compromise which is ideal to neither side and yet one with which both can live.

Divide and rule

116

Whereas the foregoing tactics apply where the supplier is faced with one customer, when there are two or more, the negotiations themselves will be far more complex. In this instance the supplier will be at a disadvantage, as his/her opponents will be able to consider the implications of what is being said and 'come back at him' from different angles. In this situation, trying to split the opposition and to do some kind of deal with one opponent which can then be used as a precedent for concluding the problems with the others may be helpful. Conversely, if they have any sense the customers here would be best advised to try to maintain a common front. Divide and rule is also dangerous if it is obvious to the parties that that is what is being attempted

1 there could be a backlash which might drive the customers into an even tighter opposition than was formerly the case and
2 the inference being given is that the opposition can be manipulated by playing one off against the other which again can generate a backlash and turn what was already an awkward encounter into a very difficult one.

Pre-emption

Whilst this is a tactic it must be stressed that this negates the concept of negotiation. Basically the concept is to make an offer to the other side which pre-empts all discussion. In other words the offer is too good to resist. Whilst this has advantages, if it is accepted, it negates the concept of the other side having an input which can create resentment.

Alternative Dispute Resolution

For really serious conflicts, where a negotiated settlement has proved impossible, rather than resorting to legal action which tends to polarise attitudes and lead to an essentially confrontational situation, recourse to Alternative Disputes Resolution (ADR) may be preferable. Under ADR both parties agree to use the offices of a mediator to settle their differences. To implement such action it may be necessary to agree the possibility of such an appointment in the initial stages of a contract, even to agreeing the name of a mediator. Whether this agreement is reached at that stage or as a result of a dispute, where both parties wish to move to a swiftly resolved settlement, a mediator is jointly appointed and jointly funded, with both parties agreeing to accept the mediator's decision as final. The mediator collects evidence from each side, considers the merits of each party's case and then makes a decision. The advantages over the legal system are:

1 saving of at least one whole set of legal expenses;
2 savings on legal costs generally;
3 saving time in considerable argument between the parties;
4 an informal and private resolution of the problem;
5 swift resolution rather than suffering the seemingly interminable delays of the legal system, and
6 less antagonistic feelings generated as a result of the dispute so that a continuation of the relationship is more likely, despite what has gone before.

A UK Centre for Disputes Resolution was set up in 1991 and in the first eighteen months of its existence dealt with business disputes worth over £550 million, whilst a Disputes panel has been set up in the City of London whereby such disputes can be resolved in front of a tribunal. Membership is by annual subscription of £400, which is deducted from the first set of fees to be charged for using the scheme. The services are available to both commercial organisations and individuals and it is possible that the panel's services will be offered on an international basis. It is anticipated that an 'instant response' service will be offered.

117

Conflagrations

Key learning points

1 Swift resolutions of complaints saves time and costs.

2 Repetition of mistakes must be avoided.

3 Where there is aggravation, tact and calmness must be employed.

4 Some complaints and complainants cannot be reconciled and may need to be countered in other ways.

Dealing with aggravation

Adopting the precepts and guidelines referred to in earlier chapters should provide a sound foundation for ensuring that the organisation is able to deal with the difficult and demanding. Using such a foundation we should be able to try to establish a rapport between parties and bring their viewpoints to some mutually acceptable compromise. If this can be achieved swiftly it may ensure that most situations can be resolved amicably. If this is not the case, not only will the resolution of the problem be difficult, but also aggravation will be caused and views may be polarised.

Case study 10.1
Repeating the error

The policy holder was assured by the representative that in making an initial lump sum investment with one of the UK's leading insurance companies should he wish to vary the manner of such investment in future he would have total flexibility. This was not so and when the policy holder changed from making lump sums to making monthly payments the company's administration became confused. The policy holder found this not only difficult to understand, since full records of the payments made were available but of considerable concern since, he reasoned if they could get that wrong, they could get other things wrong. Unfortunately the maladministration continued for several years with incorrect records of investment produced repeatedly.

Key technique

The company failed not just in their administration but in the creation or continuation of confidence in their ability to run their operation – a matter of considerable importance in view of their business and standing. The customer found his confidence in the company severely shaken as his records appeared to be more accurate than theirs. In addition, the company seemed to have little respect for his view that it was important to get things right, as it was his pension, for which he had only one opportunity to provide, which was at stake. This is another example of trying to make standard forms and letters fit all situations. If, instead of using standard letters and forms, someone had actually read and understood the problem, the company might have been able to satisfy the policy holder. This was not done and the effect was to magnify a small complaint into a major and public row, damaging to the reputation of a major company.

119

Flagging the potential problem

If there are repeated problems, it is understandable if concern turns to aggravation and elimination of the problem turns to a desire for retribution. In these circumstances, and particularly, as here, where the subject matter was an investment, problems need to be sorted out, and, above all, their repetition eliminated. Unfortunately it often seems that one mistake tends to lead to another. To combat this it should be policy that the elimination of a mistake should be overseen by a senior person and that all the implications of such a mistake should be reviewed. This could include 'flagging' customers' names so that, in the event of further contact, the matter is reviewed at a senior level and double-checked for further errors. If a customer has discovered an error and raised the matter once, then they are the type that **will**

■ check carefully on each occasion

■ bother to raise the matter, and

■ be likely to check even more carefully subsequently.

Every effort should then be made to avoid any repeat. Whereas a person may excuse mistakes the first time, a repeat will almost certainly generate outrage.

Vital though it is to obtain the facts and consider the position in all instances, nowhere is this more important than when one party is seized by anger or temper. Unfortunately, in a number of encounters such as case study 7.4, aggravation can easily develop. Temper can thwart the success of the encounter virtually out of hand. It all depends on how people are handled. Most people tend to react in the same way that they are treated, as is summed up in the following children's charter.

> The child that lives with:
>   criticism learns to condemn
>   ridicule learns to be timid
>   distrust learns to be deceitful
>   antagonism learns to be hostile.
> Conversely, the child that lives with:
>   truth learns justice
>   knowledge learns wisdom
>   patience learns to be tolerant
>   encouragement learns confidence

Figure 10.1 The children's charter (source unknown)

If we counter temper with temper, there is usually no way in which a desired result can be achieved – indeed we are likely to aggravate the situation. Conversely responding to aggravation with mildness and tact may defuse most situations, although it has to be admitted that in some instances, responding mildly can actually aggravate some awkward customers! Had the Inspector in case study 7.4 responded 'Don't you speak to me like that', the complaint could easily have developed into a row which could even have become physical. The result desired by the Inspector was to explain that he was required to inspect tickets, even if that meant some passengers then missed their train. He could afford to be sympathetic whilst not giving way as he was backed up by the 'rules' – his own instructions and the transport company's bylaws. The passenger's desired result was presumably to vent his frustration at having missed the train. Temper is not only self-defeating, it can be detrimental to one's own position, one loses control and may miss out on aspects of the case which calmer consideration might have prompted

Cases study 10.2
The animal

The company's neighbour was a car sales and service organisation and their two car parks adjoined each other. The company suffered considerably from fly parking from drivers visiting the car showrooms which had insufficient parking space. One day the Chairman found his parking space, which bore the company name, his initials and the words 'private parking', occupied by a dilapidated old car. A few minutes later, whilst the Chairman waited and fumed, the driver returned and a row broke out with considerable use of short, descriptive – but unprintable – words. The Chairman was unable to get the driver to comprehend his viewpoint, a situation which his own loss of temper did nothing to improve.

'Don't you pay any attention to the rights of others?' he fumed.

'Nah, I'm an animal.' was the stunned silence-creating reply.

121

> **Key technique**
> Nothing was gained by a loss of temper – there was no way in which any meeting of minds could be achieved here and walking away was the only practical solution. At least then the Chairman's blood pressure could resume its normal level.
> This was a case where force, by using the application of a wheel clamping arrangement advertised by bold notices, was essential to **avoid** the encounter. Indeed, the fact that the Chairman lost his temper might actually encourage the 'animal' to repeat his unsocial act!

Case study 10.3
Aggravation loses the case

Before the tribunal the consultant was confronted by his angry opposite number. The papers his opponent had sent to the tribunal had been mislaid and insufficient copies were available to allow the tribunal to sit. The angry barrister demanded that the consultant provide additional copies so that the case could proceed. The consultant, acting for the defendant, quietly pointed out that as the bundle of papers had been produced by and for the barrister, and the case had been brought by the barrister's client, the onus was surely on his side to produce replacement copies. During the very heated exchange that followed, the ire of the barrister was repeatedly countered by the icy calm of the consultant which apparently only served to aggravate the barrister's temper.

Key technique

The grip exercised by the consultant on his own rising temper played no small part in causing the barrister to lose his cool. His constant refusal to agree to demands stated as coming from 'a barrister' was apparently so much a culture shock that the barrister's grip on the case slackened and he lost.

The barrister's intention may well have been to rattle the opposition right from the start in order to try and put **them** off, or it could have been that he simply wanted someone to fight back so that a heated row could have developed. Similarly in the passenger/Inspector confrontation of case study 7.4, presumably the passenger's frustration would have been appeased had the Inspector replied in like fashion which would have given him the opportunity to 'have a go' with nothing to lose. The opportunity to bait or be rude to someone who is themself constrained by guidelines or codes of conduct appeals to some. Company representatives need to be very patient and firmly in control to avoid such a potentially dangerous situation.

Case study 10.4
Hold your breath

The client had departed on her holiday leaving the placement agency to make arrangements for a replacement *au pair* that she had selected to travel to the UK on the client's return. During the time the client was on holiday, both a former *au pair* and a neighbour contacted the agency to lodge complaints about the client. The agency could hardly ignore the complaints and decided the only thing to do was to advise the replacement *au pair* that complaints had been lodged, although it could not check their accuracy, and leave it to her to decide whether to withdraw or not. She decided to withdraw and the agency wrote to the client explaining this and returning the whole of their fee, so that the client would be free and in funds to contact other agencies. In this they went beyond the terms the client had accepted which allowed them to retain part of the fee. On her return the client was furious about the whole situation and in a state of considerable temper telephoned the agency. They tried to explain the situation calmly but the client insisted on talking over their words each time and asking rhetorical questions on which the agency refused to be drawn, simply repeating that in the circumstances they felt it would be better if she used another agency. (1) & (2)

'But you are saying you believe these people who have complained.'

'No we are not – we cannot know – we....'

'Rubbish you are believing them without asking me for my view.'

'That is not true. We had to advise...' (3)

'I find your comments insulting and patronising.'

'I'm sorry but I am trying to explain our...'

'You're explaining nothing, you are all hot air – you obviously believe the lies these people have concocted rather than believing me.'

'We cannot make such a judgement and we do not wish to...' (3)

'That's just ****, you've offered me no ******* explanation.'

'I'm sorry. I have been trying but please understand that it is difficult to explain if I can't finish explaining our points.'

'Don't be so ******* rude.' (Conversation terminated by client slamming down the telephone.)

Key techniques

(1) It seemed that the client was deliberately trying to provoke the agency into some kind of heated response which presumably would have provided a peg on which she could then hang her frustration at the developments and provide her with an edge for future action.

(2) Using rhetorical questions is a device which enables the devious to trap the unwary into statements or commitments which may be somewhat at variance to those they would make willingly. This point is examined in more detail in case study 10.5 below.

(3) The agency representative constantly tried to bring the conversation back to the facts and avoided being drawn into commenting or rebutting the client's contentions – insulting and often untrue though these were.

(4) To cover itself the agency sent a letter outlining its position and regretting that the conversation had been terminated in such an abrupt manner – quoting the actual words used by the client. The desired result as far as the agency was concerned was to extricate itself from a 'no-win' situation and, by recording aspects of the encounter in writing, which of course hardly reflected well on the client, to avoid any possibility of subsequent action.

(5) The desired result from the client's viewpoint, apart from venting

her extreme anger and frustration, is difficult to visualise. Certainly being aggressive was hardly likely to encourage the agency to retain her as a client – much the reverse. Indeed the display of anger, frustration and foul language rather supported the complaints lodged, whilst the repetition of insults made against the agency were hardly likely to endear her to them. 'Lose your temper – lose the argument' was very evident here.

The compulsive questioner

As mentioned in case study 10.4 one of the most difficult encounters can be with a customer who tries to dominate the conversation or discussion by constantly contriving statements or questions which then generate answers which assist the pre-determined plan of the questioner. Unless he is careful, the respondent will answer as the questioner intended and thus the conversation will take the contrived course. By simply reacting to the other's planned approach, the respondent loses the initiative which is the technique employed by many telephone selling organisations, for example those selling holiday timeshares.

Case study 10.5
Rhetorical question domination

Following his dismissal, the director rang a former colleague to prepare the ground for him to promote his case for reinstatement.
   'Hi, Ian, how are sales?'
   'Not too bad but obviously things are tight with this recession.'
   'I did say to you that you needed to keep sales buoyant didn't I?'
   'You did.' (1)
   'Of course you will be lacking my contacts now, and that won't help in the current recession. You'll have lost demand from them haven't you?'
   'They have been a little slow.'
   'Can't see things getting any better either – you are going to be in trouble by the end of the year unless you get sales up, aren't you?'
   'It's too early to say.' (2)
   'But every month that goes by with under budget sales is a drain on the cash flow as I said before didn't I?'
   'That's certainly true.' (3)

'I could contact my old customers and get them to place some orders for old times sake which would help, wouldn't it?' (4)

Key techniques

(1) There is little Ian can do but agree since he has been conditioned to answer. He has not broken the chain of questions which led to the ultimate 'statement question'. The fact that the former director said an innumerable number of things, which, whilst some are correct, contain much which is irrelevant and incorrect, has been overlooked.

(2) Ian's former colleague has the advantage of having prepared his 'script' for the conversation in advance, has seized the initiative and is leading it towards the desired result. Unless Ian breaks the chain an ultimate, and, on the basis of this conversation, entirely logical, 'offer' is the inevitable outcome.

(3) This rhetorical question is undeniable. However what is afoot here is that facts are being delivered in a way that seeks to bolster the accuracy and prestige of the questioner, whilst glossing over his shortcomings.

(4) With the logic built by the pre-planned conversation, the director is put in the position of virtually having to agree, particularly since any possibility of gaining an order could be helpful.

(5) In handling this kind of person it is essential to be prepared – or if thought processes are too slow compared to the swift, prepared comment/questions, to note suggestions and agree to refer back. Avoiding being trapped into an immediate response provides thinking time.

In handling this type of person and conditioning it is essential to be prepared and to remain calm whilst thinking quickly and trying to out-guess the next stage. If unable to do this then a safer solution would be to invent an excuse and say that you will ring back. The following alternative dialogue outmanoeuvres the manoeuvrer.

'Hi Ian, how are sales?'

'As we all anticipated they are slow, but we have found a number of new contacts and hope to rectify the shortfall in the near future.'

'I did say you needed to keep sales buoyant didn't I?'

'Well, there is nothing original in that is there – indeed its pretty basic at all times, isn't it?' (1)

'But every month that goes by with under budget sales is a drain on cash flow as I warned, didn't I?'

'Again that's stating the obvious – and to offset the effect we're endeavouring to chase every new contact, but obviously we are in com-

petition with a number of alternative suppliers. For that reason I can't keep chatting about it – I must get on. I'll give you a ring in a couple of weeks.' (2)

Key techniques
(1) This breaks the questioner's train of questions and reverses the rhetorical question ploy.
(2) Practising ending conversations can be helpful. In this case a swift resolution of the conversation before any offer is made may help. But even if not, at least it may retain or regain the initiative, forcing the other party into a reactive rather than proactive mode.

Making a deal under pressure

This kind of rhetorical questioning can be carried a stage further and is particularly effective where the instigator of the discussion is a complainant with a definite purpose in mind. The encounter is structured into three phases by him, although the respondent sees each phase as an individual item, and is unaware they are part of a cohesive strategy. The third party first raises a question indicating his or her preparedness to find a suitable and reasonable solution, even if it is not his own desired result. After a reasonable response or compromise has been indicated, the attitude of the party then hardens with inference of threats if that desired result is not agreed. Finally, the party moves to the third stage where a deal is suggested.

Case study 10.6
1. Persuasion 2. Threat 3. Deal

---

1. Persuasion
'I am having a few problems with this particular product but I am impressed with your organisation and I have recommended you to several contacts and I know some of them have already been in contact with you.' (1)

2. Threat
'I've been speaking to a contact in the local Trading Standards office. These problems with this product are far more serious than I thought. I understand you have received a number of other complaints of this nature – that's so isn't it?' (2)

3. Deal

'Tell you what – give me a discount on my next order with you and we'll draw a line under what's gone before and I'll keep on recommending you.' (3)

Key techniques

(1) The customer is trying to gain an edge and show that he is valuable not just for his custom but also for his contacts. The underlying hint is that the company 'owes' him, say the equivalent of a commission for gaining them additional sales.

(2) The rhetorical question is being used to force the apparently unquestionable progress to the position required, whilst reference to an outside agency is used as an attempt to generate a further edge. A robust response may be required – 'This is the first we have heard of a problem with this product – can you give us exact details please. We know of no other problems at all and fail to understand the reference to the Trading Standards office.'

(3) This is the deal. The twin edges already indicated are being used to try to gain a price advantage. The counter is to refuse firmly to allow the 'problems' – real or imagined – to be linked with the 'solution' proposed. The counter might run : 'As we have mentioned, this is the first time we have heard of a problem with this product. We would welcome full details of the difficulty so that we can consider the position and our response. A discount is hardly appropriate since if the unit is faulty surely you would want us to replace it rather than leave you with a faulty unit?'

The really demanding

Some situations can generate a loss of control, which needs to be countered. It is not an ideal start, but rather like the fabled answer given to the stranger in Ireland when asking directions to a village, 'Sure and if I were you I wouldn't start from here.', the option of an alternative start is a luxury we may not have. We usually have to deal with what we find. In the event that temper or aggression does begin to control an encounter, there may be little real point in progressing. Blood needs time to cool, and pressure to be alleviated before rational discussion can resume. Increasing blood pressure can blind some people to rational explanation or logic and often defies attempts at control, even by an impartial third party. The only person capable of re-installing a degree of control is the subject who may be the least motivated person to attempt such an act.

Case study 10.7
Boundaries

It is said that the largest numbers of disputes between neighbours concern boundaries. In this instance the row had been simmering for some time mainly, it seemed, because one mixed race family seemed to think the other was being discriminatory on racial grounds, although there was no evidence of this. The family responded to this perceived 'attitude' by insisting that the pier of a wall that had been erected before they occupied the premises, should be removed as it was encroaching on their land. The latter statement was highly questionable but they insisted very aggressively on their 'rights'. Their neighbour refused to be drawn into any conflict and refused to give way. The matter went to court and a judge adjourned the case, requesting both parties to devise some compromise solution. The aggressive neighbours continued their demands but these were quietly and repeatedly rebuffed. Eventually the parties finished up in court again where an award was made against the aggressors.

128

> **Key technique**
> Once again this was a situation where no meeting of minds was likely to occur between the parties and resolution was only possible by reference to some external source. The aggressive neighbour, like the fly parker in case study 10.2 obviously belonged to the 6 per cent of the population who are not prepared to accept a compromise and indeed see no reason for trying to compromise or get along. They have no real respect for others and it must be recognised that with these 'animals' there is really very little chance of ever being able to do a deal.

Deferral for calmness

Whilst in some instances a suggestion to defer a decision to allow calmness to return may actually worsen the situation, in most cases, a request for order matched by patience and perseverance may begin to calm the situation, as may some of the actions on the following checklist.

1 Remaining calm at all times. Once two tempers clash then it is most unlikely that any consensus will emerge and the situation will almost certainly degenerate.

2 Noting facts or opposing views without immediately commenting. Commenting hastily has no beneficial effect and may inflame the situation, whilst the longer the member, or more than one member, can talk without being challenged, the more they may be able to alleviate the pressure they feel.

3 Keeping the person(s) talking and explaining the cause of the temper loss, whilst asking neutral questions to try and uncover as much of the case, or cause of concern, as possible may help, simply through the genuine interest being evinced.

4 Attempting to further relax the person by means of refreshment, allowing smoking, or even declaring a recess or adjournment. Care should be taken not to denigrate the case being put or to infer that the dispute is not serious. The purpose of adjournment is to allow time for reconsideration, or thinking time, and not to stifle the matter.

5 The provision of refreshments, thereby diverting attention to a neutral act, may provide valuable calming time.

6 On resumption, or after the initial flow has ceased, if no adjournment has proved possible, re-check and correct the facts. This should enable a more accurate resumé of the dispute to be prepared. Further, since time will have passed since the original outburst, a more objective view may be obtained. This process can be built upon by the respondent questioning suspect facts or opinions, and challenging suppositions and claims where these appear to be unsubstantiated.

7 Leaving as much time as possible for the calming process. Points 1 to 5 may require as much as 30/40 minutes. Indeed the longer the time taken the better as the more likely it is that the temper may subside.

8 If an adjournment is possible, this should provide time to investigate the case.

9 In making a decision under pressure, care should be taken to avoid creating precedents and thus it may be preferable to make decisions of an interim nature pending final clarification and/or approval.

10 If an interim decision is agreed, a date and time should be set for review of the matter and implementation of a final decision.

Figure 10.2 Calming temper

11

A lone cowhand

Key learning points

1 Dealing on one's own creates a pressure which requires careful handling.

2 Lone operators must make positive rather than negative statements.

3 Such operators need training, guidance and supervision to ensure adherence to required procedures.

4 Staff with personal problems may need to be relieved rather than left to interface with customers.

Many complaints are lodged over the telephone or in correspondence, which is virtually inevitable where customer and supplier are remote. Whilst using the telephone is speedy and can provide an instant solution, such remote dealing loses the value of body language, which can soften and even 'explain' the true meaning of the words used. Further, some people find it far easier to be hostile or sarcastic over the telephone or in correspondence than if they are face-to-face with a real live opponent. Gaining a deal may be more likely with a face-to-face encounter than if the two parties are remote. The suggestion to 'drop in and have a chat' can go some way towards defusing problems, whilst an acceptance means that any confrontation will then take place on the supplier's home ground which may provide an edge, offer opportunities for 'a trip round the works' or allow a gift of a sample. Such relatively low cost public relations exercises can help solve difficult encounters, and are also useful customer relations devices.

Whilst such face-to-face encounters may work effectively for manufacturers since the complaint will be pursued at a private reception area or in a private office, there are dangers for some organisations where confrontations can take place in public. Indeed some demanding customers will exploit any additional profile given to their demands if they can press them in a public place.

Case study 11.1
Botching the job – publicly

The customer had bought an electrical appliance which had proved to be erratically faulty. On telephoning the store, he was told that should he bring the appliance back, it would be replaced. On taking it to the store however, the assistant who dealt with the enquiry, having given it two or three hefty slaps with his hand, indicated that if the customer left it, it would be repaired. The customer replied that was not what he had been promised on the telephone the day before and, having seen a delicate electrical item manhandled in front of his eyes he was not at all happy about having it repaired! Indeed since the fault was erratic he failed to see the point of the assistant's action. (1)

He requested he be able to see the manager, but instead a supervisor was called:

'*Good morning sir, what seems to be the problem?*' (2)

'*Basically this product is only a month old and is intermittently faulty – I rang to find out what I should do – return it to the manufacturer or to you and was told to bring it in and you would replace it. Your assistant hit it several times with his hand and told me I can leave it for repair which I find entirely unsatisfactory.*'

'*Well that is our policy, sir.*'

'*But it is not what it says on your guarantee – it says here you will replace any items found to be faulty within three months of purchase.*'

'*I am afraid that is not our current guarantee, sir.*' (3)

'*But it's the one you supplied with this product – it says here under your company's name that you will replace, I was told on the telephone you would replace and I have brought it in – making a special 20 mile journey – for it to be replaced.*'

'*I see – could I show that guarantee to the manager, sir?*'

The supervisor took the guarantee and went to see the manager – not returning for 10 minutes.

'*I am sorry sir, the manager is not around and I can't find anyone in a position to make a decision.*' (4)

'*With all due respect that is not my fault – I have made a special trip here, following phoning you for advice yesterday. I must insist you replace this faulty item, or I will have to take this matter up with the Trading Stan-*

131

dards officer and, since I am a shareholder, with your Board of Directors.'
'Let me try again to see if I can contact the manager, sir.' (5)

Key techniques

(1) This encounter took place on the shop floor surrounded by customers, several of whom not only saw the item being manhandled by the assistant which was hardly a good recommendation for the way the store treated its products, but then hung around to hear the rest of the event, in one or two cases giving moral support to the customer.
(2) The supervisor must have been aware of the high-profile situation of the complaint. By starting positively she attempted to defuse the situation, only to be let down by the non-appearance of management.
(3) Whilst a swift solution to the situation could have worked, indeed could have been good public relations for the onlookers, it might have been better for the supervisor to have tried to move the encounter to a more private place. By raising his voice the customer could involve other customers in the dialogue and create additional pressure on the store staff.

This is another example of the need to get the terms of business right:

- Had the correct guarantee been provided, the case of the customer would have been severely weakened.

- Had the telephonist given the correct advice, the encounter might either have been avoided or been far less demanding and confrontational.

(4) You can cover a great deal of a relatively small store in 10 minutes and it defies belief that it took all this time to find that the manager was not around.
(5) Whilst it is difficult to judge whether the supervisor had made the decision on her own, or whether management reversed its instructions to her, and whether it was just coincidence that the customer had announced that he was a shareholder or not, the customer achieved his desired result. The same can hardly be said for the retailer – the hiatus was witnessed by several customers and there was potential damage to the reputation of this national chain. The patience and professionalism of the supervisor was the one saving grace.

Case study 11.2
Cashless transaction

The owner of two small businesses banked at a central London branch but had arrangements to cash cheques at his local branch. On visiting the branch one lunchtime he found it very busy, although few cashiers were operating. When he eventually got to the counter he was served by a new cashier whom he did not know. He presented the cheque and explained that there was an arrangement to cash it.

'I'm sorry sir but I can't find any record of the arrangement.'

'I appreciate you are new and don't know me but I have had cashing arrangements on my business accounts here for the last seven years and use them roughly every other week.'

'I'm awfully sorry sir but I can't cash this cheque without authority.'

'Is the manager around?'

'Sorry sir, he is at lunch.'

'The under manager then.'

'She's on holiday this week.'

'So basically until the manager returns from lunch or you find the arrangement authority you can't cash my cheque?'

'Yes sir – could you come back later?'

> **Key technique**
> Once again this was an instance where the basic training of staff was faulty. The arrangement confirmation was in the branch where it had been for seven years but no-one had shown the newcomer where it was.

It would be reasonable to think, given the adverse publicity to which the banking profession in the UK has been subject recently, that every effort would have been made to improve customer service, and to introduce fail-safe systems particularly for private and small business customers who often have alternative methods of banking and who are the foundation and backbone of most banks. The UK banking system has had an Ombudsman service since 1986. In his report for 1993, the Ombudsman, Lawrence Shurman, was highly critical of the attitude of banks generally to their customers and, in particular to their 'mean-spirited' approach to dealing with customer complaints. If that is how banks seek to deal initially with complaints, many of which will be found to be entirely justified, this will almost inevitably lead to the creation of demanding customers where only concerned individuals

133

formerly existed. As the Ombudsman commented 'Banks will put mistakes right, but they are less willing to apologise. Yet often what the customer is looking for is a prompt and unreserved apology. If he gets one I find that all too frequently it will be grudging or belated – or both'.

Case study 11.3
Saying 'Yes'

Not all banks find it difficult to apologise. In December 1993 the story of one customer's dispute with the TSB made national press headlines. It had been shown that the bank had made a mistake regarding the operation of a customer's account and as a result the customer had been forced to undertake a considerable amount of correspondence to correct the mistake. When he was offered compensation for the mistake he felt it was insufficient and invoiced the Bank for the several letters he had been forced to write to clarify the matter. Much to the credit of the TSB they agreed to pay the charge he levied, stating in a covering letter 'You are not expecting too much from any major high street bank to deal with any concern raised as speedily as possible'.

> **Key technique**
> No doubt this does create a precedent but it should also provide a lesson. In this case the charge was levied because the initial complaint had not been dealt with satisfactorily and promptly. If suppliers are to be held liable for charges from customers for sorting out problems they have caused, this may be the best way of drawing attention to the need for proper customer care, thereby improving standards and avoiding demanding customers.

To the outsider it seems that some banks' response to their loss-making strategies of the 70s and 80s has been to increase charges to their long-suffering customers and to cut costs. Some cost-cutting has been achieved by removing supervision that could handle difficult customer problems so that young inexperienced staff often with little empathy for the customers, as well as less commitment than their predecessors, are placed at the cutting edge. Many such staff seem either unable or unwilling to say 'I'm sorry' but will try to explain away or defend the indefensible.

Case study 11.4
Liar
___

The customer operated a number of accounts with one of the top four UK clearing banks from which bankers' orders were paid. He wrote to the bank cancelling an order made from one of these accounts specifying all relevant details. Some weeks later he was horrified to receive from his insurers a note that as he had missed paying a premium, one of his life policies was being suspended.

He contacted the bank and explained the situation.
  'I expect they've lost it.' was the initial reply from a young clerk.
  'I think that's unlikely – don't you think you should check first to see whether you paid it?'
  'Oh OK – I'll ring you back.'
48 hours later when no call had been received the customer rang the bank again.

  'No, we haven't paid that premium – we cancelled it in accordance with your instructions.'
  'What instructions?'
  'The instructions you sent us some weeks ago.'
  'I think you will find if you check that what you have done is to cancel the wrong premium from the wrong account.'
  'No, we haven't done that.'
  'I'm sorry but you must have done – it's the only explanation.'
  'No, that's impossible.'
  'OK – please send my statements on all three accounts today.'

When the statements arrived they showed plainly that indeed the wrong premium from the wrong account had been cancelled. The customer wrote pointing out that although he accepted that mistakes could happen, the clerk concerned had been both off-hand, not bothered to check the details, suggested the customer take action to correct the bank's fault and had lied into the bargain.

___
Remedial actions
(1) The prime consideration of the clerk should have been to apologise and then to have checked all the data carefully. Had he done so the mistake should have been obvious.

(2) Whether someone as inexperienced or as apparently untrained should have been placed in the position of dealing with customers is questionable.

> (3) It might be preferable to have one trained and experienced member of staff dedicated to solving such problems.

Failure to solve disputes at a local level not only leads in many cases to more senior staff being involved internally, but can also mean that the dispute moves into the public arena as was the case with the TSB in case study 11.3. The Ombudsman's office even has the power to intervene and to award compensation. Given the level of discontent evidenced by the Ombudsman's figure, it is hardly surprising that non-branch banking has made so much headway so quickly – clear evidence that if an industry is unable to deal effectively with disputes the effects of long term change may be forced upon it if a competitor gets it right. As noted earlier, the non-branch banking operation spends a great deal on training its staff who can only interface via the telephone but nevertheless seem able to empathise with their account-holders far better than can their competitors who have the benefit of face-to-face encounters. Such competition is likely to pose considerable problems for the traditional banking operation. In the USA, 15 per cent of customers already use such a system, whereas in the UK it is estimated that by the end of the century no less than 6 000 000 people (20 per cent of the banking population) will bank by telephone.

Lone operators

In two of these case studies employees were left to fend for themselves. Normally more senior personnel might have been available for help, but to one section of personnel this luxury is never available. Many employees have to operate remote from home base, for example in a customer's own premises. In such situations there is rarely any back up available. If the receptionists at Reading Borough Council (see Chapter 7) find themselves in difficulties in refusing to let a visitor or caller speak to a member of the Council staff, presumably there is a more senior person on hand to field the problem. However in the field, representatives, fitters and repairers, and advisers operate on their own where there is little or no direct supervision. It is arguable that those who travel around as a sole representative of their organisation need greater support and training than any other personnel, since:
1 They have to deal face-to-face with the customer.
2 They will be dealing with the customer on his or her own ground which may put them at a disadvantage.

3 They need to know their product and all the problems associated with the product, not just to deal with the fault, but to provide reassurance to the customer.
4 They lack recourse to senior personnel for assistance or another viewpoint.

Passing the buck

It is perhaps hardly surprising if, in order to evade responsibility some take refuge in shifting the blame – either to another person or on to the product, neither of which is in the interests of the company.

Case study 11.5
Always the other bloke...

When the fitter called to mend the washing machine, he was confronted by an irate householder who pointed out that his colleague had only serviced the machine two days earlier, since when it had performed more poorly than had been the case prior to the service. Having carried out an inspection and the repair, the fitter commented that the previous job had not been done very well and this was because the company was sending people out with insufficient training.

Key technique
'Rubbishing the company' may have been a reasonable personal ploy to divert the customer's ire, and to win a cup of tea, but it is the last way of answering a complaint that the company would have wished.

Remedial actions
To combat this type of adverse public relations:
(1) Adopt a policy of using follow up evaluations of such visits asking the customer for their impression of the service and the person, and making it known that this will occur. Or
(2) Train the person to 'conceal' any previous poor work. Thus in the above example the fitter should have been entirely non-committal until he had seen the machine – simply apologising in the first place. After looking at the trouble he might have used a form of wording such as:
'I am so sorry that we weren't able to fix your machine in one try. I can see what the trouble is and I can understand why it wasn't cured before. It is quite difficult to adjust the grommet so that it operates reli-

ably. I think I have fixed it now – but if you have any further trouble don't hesitate to contact us again – obviously we will not charge you for this visit, and as I've also tightened up the widget, you should find the machine works much better than it did before.' To create a 'feel good' empathy a few white lies may be preferable to rubbishing the other fitter, the effect of which is to damage not only that person's reputation but also that of the company.

Case study 11.6
The problem is really this lousy machine

The repairman kept sighing as he attempted to repair the laser printer. 'Oh these blooming Mark Three Bloggitt printers – they're useless you know – always breaking down, completely unreliable. The trouble we have with these you wouldn't believe, they're nowhere near as good as the old Mark Two model. I really don't know why they had to change from the old model.'

138

Key techniques
(1) This could be called the 'biting the hand that feeds you' syndrome as the repairer is rubbishing the product which it is his job to repair. Indeed, if the machines did not need repairing he would be out of a job, whilst if he didn't like repairing them, why do the job?
(2) The repairer should be trained to be positive about the machine stressing its good points and glossing over the problems of the breakdown or repair required. He needs to be reminded that to those people with whom he interfaces, he **is** the company. If he is critical of the products it says very little for either product or company. Such criticism immediately begs the customer's question 'if it is so bad why do you work for them?'

Remedial action
Explaining the above reactions may induce a more positive response.

Case study 11.7
The problem is the client

The service engineer had been called to tend to the photocopier which had developed a fault and was printing copies with a line running down the page from top to bottom. On seeing it, the service engineer commented that it was almost certainly the owner's fault as she had probably put a paper clip into the machine. The client was irate not so much for the fact that her own sense was being called into question – that is that she would put paper bearing a paper clip through the machine, as for the fact that she was being asked to believe it would be possible for a paper clip to enter the works. She felt the service engineer was patronising her as a woman who did not understand machinery, and complained to the Head Office.

Key technique

This comes under the classification of the complaint that need never have been. It was obvious to all except the service engineer that the fault lay within the refill cartridge but because such a thing had not happened before, he failed to keep an open mind and made an assumption thereby aggravating the whole situation. Had he confessed to being completely baffled as to the cause, this could have been understood by the client and even sympathised with. Once the problem had been resolved with a replacement cartridge, which eventually removed the line, the matter would have been closed. Instead of which the dispute rumbled on with eventually an apology being needed from the Managing Director to avoid a far more public row with overtones of sexual discrimination.

139

None of the scenarios outlined in these last few case studies should have happened – but they do, regularly. Checking on the attitude, behaviour and competence of the 'lone cowhand' employee should be regarded as the minimum effort required to monitor such work. Thus, following a service of a gas boiler, British Gas ask their customers to complete a fairly detailed questionnaire about the way in which the service was carried out. Were comments such as those highlighted above to be made, there would be an opportunity for this to be reported back and action taken. With such a commitment to better and more reliable service, it would be churlish to criticise companies using the questionnaire approach, although it always amuses me to be asked to indicate whether the work was done 'properly' – as a non-engineer how can I judge?

Ideally a telephoned or personal visit check-up would be the best way to ensure that the service provided is in accordance with the policy adopted by the company. Relatively few organisations actually do this, although some require supervisors to spot check their employees by attending a service.

Temper

Lone operators may often experience temper generated by frustration. Thus in case study 11.5 one could understand if not condone the real anger of the householder, needing to call back a repairer within 48 hours of an earlier repair which should have rectified the problem. Faced with anger the repairman would need to operate very carefully as saying the wrong word, or even any word, could exacerbate the situation. The best solution here would be to say as little as possible – perhaps explaining as tactfully as possible that, at least whilst doing the repair, he needs to concentrate. Whilst involved in the repair itself, either feigning difficulty of hearing, or needing to concentrate might also help play for time, hoping that time itself will assist the dissipation of the anger. By far the best solution is to keep apologising. Even if the apology is not thought to be merited what does it cost? They say that 'talk is cheap' and indeed it is, but the effect of apparently sincere apologies can be very valuable in defusing these potentially difficult situations. It is literally a case of 'if you can fake sincerity, you've got it made' – a rule that should perhaps be the motto of all customer care operations, although real sincerity is a preferable aim and usually distinguishable from a 'put on'.

Alternatively, and preferably in addition to an apology, the operator could suggest that the customer should contact the office, providing a telephone number and named respondent. If the respondent is a dedicated 'complaint dealer', suitable responses will be automatic when such a call comes in. The compiling of a form to be given to customers allowing them to record their concerns before forwarding it for consideration by a supervisor may also assist in defusing such situations.

Personal problems

The last difficulty we should highlight for lone operators is their need to relate positively at all times even when personal problems may be threatening to overcome their judgement and ability to deal effectively. When needing to deal with problems in house, if an employee's personal problems are affecting performance, another respondent may be able to take over. This may not be possible with the lone operator.

It has been estimated that at any one time up to one-fifth of an organisation's workforce will have a personal problem likely to affect their performance. Of these just under 40 per cent (or around 10 per cent of the total workforce) will be experiencing a serious problem – divorce, death or serious illness of a close relative or friend, court case, and so on. Stress-related illnesses accounted for over a third of certified absence in the UK in 1991. Cutting staff because of the recession, an ageing workforce as well as a general decline in health have been put forward as reasons for what has been a considerable rise in stress-related illnesses. The reasons, whilst important in their own context, are irrelevant here; what concerns us is the effect on our businesses of putting employees suffering from personal problems and/or stress into the firing line of dealing with demanding customers, which may itself aggravate the stress to the detriment of the public face of the business, as well as that of the employee.

Case study 11.8
Fuelling her problems   141

The driver at the petrol station was very annoyed since he felt the cashier had been most offhand to him. At the end of the protracted transaction he remarked to the cashier that she should be careful as her attitude could offend customers. He was so concerned that he complained to the company operating the service station and was told that earlier in her shift the cashier had been told that the company were making her redundant.

Key technique
It is hardly surprising if problems are generated or aggravated if lone operator staff are left to cope in such circumstances. Suitable cover should be been provided or the delivery of the information delayed until the end of the cashier's shift.

In a 1993 report for the Health and Safety at Work Executive, Professor Tom Cox of Nottingham University recommended that stress at work, which it is estimated costs 90 million lost working days in the UK each year, should be regarded as a health and safety issue. In addition to the cost of the productive days lost, the potential extra damage to an employer's business if employees suffering from stress are required to try to cope with difficult customers can be considerable.

12

Damage limitation

> **Key learning points**
>
> 1 Public utterances must be examined for unintended meanings or effects.
>
> 2 Failing to deal with complaints in-house can lead to external interest and potentially damaging publicity.
>
> 3 Disaster and contingency planning is essential to minimise the effect of such an occurrence on the business.
>
> 4 When customers are injured the added dimension of insurer's interests must not be overlooked.

Public image

So far we have considered complaint encounters that have been contained within the circle of customer and supplier. However there may be a need to deal with demanding customers in the full glare of the public spotlight – in public places, *via* public utterances and/or interviews, or in the aftermath of disasters. Sadly those required to operate in such circumstances do not always appreciate the implications of what they have to say.

Case study 12.1
Calamity was a four letter word

In making a presentation in November 1990 to the Institute of Directors, Gerald Ratner, then Chairman of the company which he had successfully built into one of the largest jewellery retailers in the world, wished to make an effect and impress his comments on the delegates. He humorously compared some of his products to human waste and added that there was more value in a Marks and Spencer prawn sandwich than in some products his shops sold. His humorous intent and the context of his remarks were forgotten in the mass reporting of his words which had a calamitous effect on the whole UK chain. Sales slumped and so did the share price (from 177p to 8p). Ratner himself had to give up the Chairmanship and resign as a director. The combination of the effects of his remark and the UK recession led to the closing of over 350 shops and even to the change of the company name.

Key technique
'Never rubbish the product' is one of the key learning phrases drilled into every salesperson's head. Here not only were the products rubbished, but so too were the customers themselves. Ignore the fact that the remark was not meant to be taken seriously and that it was reported out of context, the point was that those customers who were considering buying in the critical run up to Christmas, thought again, and bought elsewhere. Inferring the products had little value brought into question the customers' taste.

Remedial action
Every public utterance needs to be carefully assessed. Those required to interface with the media, or in public, need to be coached in this role.

143

In case study 12.1 the real problem caused was that of unintentionally ridiculing the customers in a very public arena. The public dimension should be carefully borne in mind at all times yet, strangely, is often overlooked.

Case study 12.2
No answer = no sale

The supplier sent out a 'cold sell' mail shot for a personalised diary. Due to a mix-up in the mailing process one prospective customer was sent a diary personalised for another person. As requested he returned the slip asking for more details and added that he did not have the sample promised as he had been sent that generated for another. No answer was received.

At a conference surrounded by delegates he met the supplier who was enthusing about the product which the customer agreed was very good value and in which he had been very interested. 'Why didn't you buy it then?' asked the supplier. 'Why didn't you answer my letter?' came the swift reply. 'As you didn't answer, I didn't order.'

Key technique

No amount of apologising could then make the customer change his mind, as, to the customer, the supplier had had his chance and 'blown it'. To aggravate the problem, the setting for the confrontation was very public.

Remedial action

If correspondence should be acknowledged within 24 hours and answered within 15 days, then queries and/or complaints, particularly where these seem to relate to mistakes emanating from the organisation, should be given priority, perhaps requiring an answer within three days.

Prompt and adequate response is required from organisations that have a public profile in order to avoid, or at least minimise, the possibility of adverse publicity as one never knows what strings the customer may have to pull.

144

Case study 12.3
Please (don't) join us!

The customer regularly used one of a chain of motels and noticed an invitation for guests to apply for the operating company's credit card to gain free priority booking. He applied and found to his annoyance that his application was rejected. He rang the credit company to query the position.

'I'm sorry I am not allowed to go into details concerning applications for the cards.'

'I don't find that acceptable – I want to know a reason for this decision.'

'I am sorry I cannot disclose that – I cannot say more.'

'Are you saying that following your inviting my application for the card, and my having completed the application, you reject it and are not prepared to state the reason?'

'I am afraid so.'

'Please tell me immediately the credit checking company you use'. (1)

[Later] *'I have checked my credit rating with the company you use and it is impeccable. In the circumstances I cannot see why you have not accepted the application – do you have anything to add?'*

'No, I am sorry we cannot enter into discussion regarding individual applications.'

'But why do you invite applications if you then ignore them?'

'I really cannot comment.'

> **Key techniques**
> (1) If low usage or some other factor ruled out granting a card, this should have been made clear on the application form. Inviting application and then rejecting it without explanation is not only damaging to the reputation of the company but is simply a means of generating difficult encounters.
> (2) The traveller considered buying shares in the company and then attending the public Annual General Meeting which was always well attended by the national press, to gain an opportunity of publicly airing his grievance.

In high profile encounters what is at stake is the reputation of the organisation – a reputation that can take years to build and just a few seconds adverse publicity to destroy.

Adverse publicity

145

Public investigations provide consumers with a lever to be used if they feel the organisation is not granting the respect they feel is merited by their complaint or request. However there are other ways in which publicity is given to the operations of the company and damage can be done to its reputation, leading to a situation where customers can become demanding, or even, where instead of demands being aggravated, sales demand is stifled, by a simple lack of forethought.

Case study 12.4
Begging the question

In September 1992, considerable media attention was focussed on chairmen and chief executives of certain organisations, particularly monopolistic former public corporations, who were awarding themselves remuneration apparently out of proportion to their responsibilities and to those holding comparable positions in other organisations. A number of company chairmen were interviewed for the BBC television programme Panorama which carried out a lengthy investigation into the subject. The interviewees included a chairman of a recently privatised utility who obviously resented being called to account for the hefty increase in his own salary. The more evasive he became, the more pressing became the interviewer to the point where the Chairman decided to end the interview by walking off the set. He rose but continued an increasingly heated exchange with the interviewer, all of which was caught by the camera and subsequently screened.

Key techniques

Leaving aside the loss of face occasioned by the display of temper and the loss of reputation occasioned by such a public examination, the Chairman failed in the fundamentals of the interview situation:

(1) Apparently neither he, nor his staff, had taken the trouble to construct suitable answers or defences to anticipated questions. One must assume he knew the subject under review, as a programme with such a reputation is unlikely to have misled him, and thus knew that he was likely to be quizzed on his own pay situation. With this knowledge a suitable defence should have been constructed. This might not have been too convincing but it would at least have provided some defence or explanation.

(2) His staff should have prepared him for the intrusive questioning technique, coached him in retaining his good humour and avoiding a situation where he was seen to lose his temper.

(3) He should have been made aware that simply replying 'No comment' whilst being in no way a satisfactory answer, would have avoided him being caught on screen trying to disentangle himself from the microphone to leave the studio. Refusing to answer questions makes boring viewing and the producer would have been forced to cut the interview short – or not even to have used it. Being embroiled in a heated exchange with the interviewer was, by contrast, compulsive, if embarrassing, viewing.

(4) He should have remembered the adage 'Lose your temper – lose the argument'. Being seen to run away from the question immediately implied that he had no defence or explanation to offer. In the circumstances viewers, some of whom were shareholders in the company, could hardly have concluded other than that his remuneration might be high.

Remedial action

As well as researching the tactics used by the interviewer, the interviewee needs to be in command of details of all previous comments made by the organisation on the subject matter. This may entail some lengthy research and cross-referencing, but it is vital to ensure that there is no contradiction of what has gone before, or if there is, that the reason for such change is known, and the interviewee has a ready explanation. Being fazed by such a question will leave the interviewee floundering and provide a negative impression of both spokesperson and organisation. Here one could understand shareholders raising questions at a subsequent Annual General Meeting, or confidence being lost in the ability of the board.

Catastrophe

In terms of customer satisfaction, investigations like the *Sunday Times* 'Questions of cash' column referred to in case study 13.3 are valuable assets as they provide a lever to individual customers who become frustrated at their lack of power to bring suppliers to book. This 'good guy' status cannot always be claimed by the media, as the way in which it builds concepts, products and even personalities, only to turn on them and damage or destroy them may help them improve their circulation figures but can be disastrous for the subject product or organisation. 'If you want peace prepare for war' runs the old saying and nowhere is this more apt than in relation to disaster or contingency planning. The concept embraces the principle that it is preferable to consider alternative actions and reactions before a disaster occurs, to doing so in the immediate aftermath when the disaster sets in train a sequence of events which have a momentum of their own, and require answers to some very demanding questions. Not only does the organisation need an instant response to get its operations back into gear but, almost inevitably, disasters tend to have a high public profile, thus resulting in media, customer, and even public interest which must be dealt with positively. The slightest indication of lack of preparedness or confidence can swiftly exacerbate an already difficult position.

147

Case study 12.5
Disaster effects

1) The Union Carbide disaster in Bhopal, India, sparked a considerable public interest in the safety of chemical plants, particularly from those living near such a plant in the UK. This led to the UK chemical industry trade association setting up a well-briefed information desk able to deal with a flood of enquiries from members of the public as well as from the media.

In the absence of such information customers, neighbours and members of the public could have combined as a potential negative force against chemical works, and their products. By advance attention, the Association saved its members from a potentially large number of demanding encounters.

2) British Midland won considerable praise for the way it coped with the aftermath of the M1 air crash. Such well-managed, detailed response and reaction was not instinctive but the result of planning for such an eventuality. Planning, which it was hoped would never be used, paid off to the benefit of the company's reputation when the unwanted occurred. When concerned families and customers rang the airline in their hundreds, the response was positive, reassuring and professional. An inability to respond, too many 'don't know' answers, or an amateurish response could have completed a process of confidence-destruction in the airline which the crash had started. As it was, despite the tragedy, the reputation of the airline was enhanced.

3) In late 1991, SmithKline Beecham (SKB), makers of Lucozade, were the target of alleged product tampering by the Animal Liberation Front. Not only were 5 000 000 bottles of Lucozade removed from retail outlets and destroyed, but the telephone line that the company set up to deal with enquiries handled over 1 500 calls, including only one from a person complaining of feeling unwell. To give this type of response there needed to be complete and detailed response plans prepared with trained staff ready to answer enquiries and complaints in a tactful yet responsive manner. Any failure to deal with the calls in a positive and professional manner could have destroyed the reputation of the company.

Responding to crises like these requires preparation and research and a commitment of resources in advance and anticipation of the problem. Training those responsible for dealing with the enquiries takes time and resources. Any hesitation or unsure tone or inflection in the voice can worry rather than re-assure. In addition, the automatic answer to some questions may beg other questions and thus the questions, and their suggested answers, need to be reviewed from a number of angles.

Wanted – a devil's advocate

To ensure the answers provided are as honest as possible and can legitimately boost or restore confidence, it is essential to try and imagine all the worst questions including those an organisation sincerely hopes will never be asked. Playing the devil's advocate in this way, seeking as wide a source of questions as possible, should not only provide a comprehensive list of questions but should also prompt consideration and improvement, of many of the current administrative procedures.

Double-edging – the devil's alternative

In dealing with queries regarding Lucozade, no doubt SKB was asked why it was removing product from the shops. Presumably, the enquirers could have been told that the company either thought they had been contaminated and were removing contaminated product, or that they had not been contaminated but were checking all the same. Even the further alternative – that this was merely a precautionary exercise, almost invites the comment, that presumably the company's wrapping was not tamper proof! To ensure that concern or irritation does not become aggravated into a more serious and difficult situation merely by default or accident, those placed in the position of responding to queries need to be trained to consider the effect of every word.

149

In case study 12.7 below, the agency might be tempted to reply to the criticism made by the client, that it had formed the opinion that the situation within his family was not such that was suitable for a visitor. However that immediately begs the statement 'If you thought that, either you should have said so, or you should not have placed her with the family'. Either way, an attacking response to the answer to the family's criticism could easily rebound.

Those responsible for making public utterances need to weigh and consider the effect of every word, especially those that may have an emotive sense.

Case study 12.6
Water problems

The consumer noticed that his mains tap water seemed very cloudy. He let the water run and examined it again, using a long glass so that he could see more clearly. The water remained very cloudy. Bearing in mind that there had been a number of problems in the London area with water supplies being infected by toxic organisms, he rang the emergency number for the water company.

'Our water supply seems to be very cloudy.'

'Have you tried running the tap for some time?'

'Yes, and it is still the same.'

'Our workmen have been in your area today so it is probably air in the water.'

'Would air make the supply cloudy?'

'It could do – but there's no need to panic.'

Key technique

The water company spokesperson had not been properly briefed in the terms of the use of certain words in communicating with customers. Here 'panic' was both inaccurate and inadvisable since:

■ it brought an instinctive and negative reaction from a consumer who was, he thought, sensibly bringing the problem to the attention of the utility concerned, and

■ the word itself is emotive and could create a feeling that the situation really was more serious than it was, one where panic might perhaps be appropriate! For the supplier to infer the customer was panicking is patronising and rude, even if unintentional.

Remedial action

Train those placed in such a position to consider their words carefully and to appreciate the effect of emotive words on their listener.

Since many of these questions have double-edged answers, the full implications of each answer need to be considered. Whilst 'no comment' is a safe and useful answer in some rare situations, such as the interview referred to in case study 12.4, it is not particularly helpful, especially if there is a question demanding an answer.

The public profile

Although many organisations have a public profile in terms of potential media interest, some have an additional profile because they need to operate under licence issued by a governmental body, or in accordance with guidelines issued by such a body which gives them an exposure to public threat that non-licensed bodies do not experience.

Case study 12.7
Threats

Au pair placement agencies operate under guidelines issued by the Home Office and (until 1994) in accordance with licences issued by the Department of Employment.

'I understand that the au pair *you placed with my family three months ago left today.'*

'So I believe.'

'I want to know what you are going to do about it.'

'I am sorry, but I am sure you know from our terms there is nothing more we can do.'

'But that's not good enough – she should be here, instead of which she's waltzed off, leaving us in the lurch for no apparent reason.'

'I'm not sure if that is quite right, as she told me earlier that, not for the first time, you and she had a serious argument and because she is so frightened of you, she couldn't bear to remain in the house.'

'I'm not having that – she is supposed to be here with my family – I intend taking this up with the Home Office and the Department of Employment.'

'I see.'

'What do you say to that?'

'I really have no comment. Obviously you have a right to take the matter up with whomever you wish. If they ask us for comments – we will have to state what we know.'

'And that is...?'

'What both parties have told us.'

'And you will then decide who is right – as you have done already?'

'Not at all – we try not to take sides as we are not in your house and only know what happens secondhand.'

'Well, I am going to report this to the Home Office and Department of Employment.'

'As I have said – you have every right to take any such action you deem fit.'

151

Key techniques

(1) The client is seeking to use the reference to 'official' bodies as a threat. The calm response may have two effects – a) to cool the complainant down and allow more rational thought and consideration, and, b) to infer that, since the organisation is apparently not worried about

> such referral, the client will be wasting his time.
> (2) Making a suggestion that the client should desist from such report-
> ing, even if there were concern at the idea, could be an indication of
> weakness and provide an edge or lever for the client to try to gain
> some consideration or compensation.

Customer injury

Most of the case studies in this chapter highlight the difficult encounters that can be created by a careless approach. In seeking to minimise such damage and the incidence of such encounters, however, we
must not overlook situations where, despite our own inclinations, we
may be unable to deal effectively or take action with the degree of
flexibility we would otherwise wish. For example the 'dealing' situation becomes far more complicated when injury has been caused to a
customer, as the interests of the company *vis-à-vis* its good name
within the public arena and its own wish to be seen to be doing the
right thing, can clash with the interests of its Public Liability insurers who will be concerned that nothing should be done or said to indicate an acceptance of liability which could prejudice them from
subsequently avoiding liability. In this event the organisation needs
to clear with its insurers what can be done and said, since there will
be public pressure, perceived or real, for it to take some action.

152

Case study 12.8
The liability problem

An elderly lady tripped over a delivery box left in an aisle in a shop and
broke her wrist. The shop had a high profile locally and the management,
apart from its own genuine concern for the lady, wanted to be seen to be
acting in the best possible way, although they were aware of the interest
of their public liability insurers. Accordingly, they sent a bouquet of
flowers and a box of chocolates from the shop staff, rather than from the
company that owned the shop, with a note, again from the staff in their
personal capacity, wishing her a speedy recovery. The shop manageress
checked regularly with the lady's family on her progress. In every contact
very neutral language was used.

> **Key technique**
> The conflicting interests of the shop's high public profile and genuine concern for an injured customer, and its insurers' aversion to any such act must be considered and reconciled. The standard wording in such an eventuality is 'Without prejudice', which indicates that such a document or its content cannot be used in court, although one can hardly write that on the wrapping of a bouquet of flowers or box of chocolates!

In this instance no written communication or face-to-face encounter took place. In fact, no action was ever taken, as the lady made a good recovery, and she and her family were very appreciative of the sincere interest and good wishes of the shop staff.

Takeover

153

Similar problems arise should an organisation be under public scrutiny as a result, for example, of a takeover bid. Here, again, the capacity of an organisation to deal may be limited from forces outside its control.

Case study 12.9
Oh no you can't

Just before Christmas a takeover bid was launched by a private individual and rejected as opportunistic and hostile by the company. Within a few days, representatives of the predator tried to gain access to and information concerning many of the company outlets claiming that 'they were taking over' and needed the information to plan ahead. Fortunately the company had procedures that set out what retail staff should do in such circumstances and politely replied that it was against 'company policy' to allow access or give information. Under pressure the staff simply and politely referred all enquirers to head office.

> **Key technique**
> If one replies 'I can't let you' the personalisation of the reply allows the opponent to try to coerce the apparent authority to change his or her mind. Referring to some absent authority de-personalises the affair and allows the face-to-face encounter to remain good humoured despite the answer being the same!

Knowing the organisation faces takeover can have a marked effect on the attitude of those who interface directly with customers and their normal, and hopefully positive, manner of dealing may be impaired. Once a takeover bid is launched, most employees will assume the worst and a belief that their job is at stake is an inevitable distraction from the day-to-day customer relations problems. As already noted, employees under stress are not best placed to deal with problems. Once the public became aware of the content of the speech referred to in case study 12.1, there was considerable comment in the shops, some of it adverse. In such a situation the most patient assistant can perhaps be excused for becoming a little sharp when the subject is referred to for the twentieth time. However, understandable it may be – it still needs to be guarded against.

Trying it on

Key learning points

1 Adopting relationship tactics will reduce the incidence of demanding encounters.

2 Keeping it simple and dealing swiftly are ideal criteria.

3 Not all complaints are justified. Some 'complaints' need to be resisted.

4 The detection of false claims can be effected by using cross-referencing and computer technology.

155

A basic approach

Following the guidelines outlined in sharp end SARAH, (see Chapter 7) should help us generate progress towards our desired outcome – the resolution of the complaint. However, SARAH must be used positively. If we simply 'go through the motions' of applying a procedure without enthusiasm for the action, this can communicate itself to the other party and actually impair the likelihood of success in moving towards the desired outcome. In other words, we can adopt all the practical procedures and use negotiating tactics for as long as we like, yet we can still fail if the other side suspects that we are not sincere in our endeavours. As stated before: 'Fake sincerity and you've got it made'. This does not advocate insincerity but suggests that in trying to 'deal' the appearance of sincerity or genuine concern, even if not present, will assist in achieving the desired outcome.

Smile

A smile will encourage the other party to relax. Many people view lodging a complaint with some trepidation and expect an aggressive response. Being greeted by a smiling face should help allay such fears as well as aiding the flow of information which is the first step towards finding a solution. It is difficult to be rude to someone who is smiling and trying to be helpful. The effect of a smile can be disarming.

A smile can also indicate an apparent concern to ensure that things are rectified. Often complaints are aggravated simply because an off-hand response indicates to the customer that there is a total lack of real concern for the customer's problem, exactly the problem in case study 2.3.

Case study 13.1
Smile, smile, smile

An article in the *Financial Times* in October 1993 illustrated the value of encouraging employees to smile and to be welcoming to customers. Harrington Caravans, based in the Delamere Forest in Cheshire, believe that a customer's first impressions of a company are all important and encourage all their employees to greet customers with a smile and a 'Good morning'. Similarly the former owner of a garden centre in Chester-le-Street, County Durham insisted that his staff, despite the fact that their tasks often required them to look down in tending plants and so on, should look up and greet customers. Echoing comments repeatedly made here and in particular the philosophies exemplified in case studies 3.6 and 3.7, regular FT columnist Charles Batchelor commented 'The benefits of these efforts should appear in loyal customers, who, over the years, will spend large sums with the company. Existing customers are far easier and cheaper to reach than new ones whilst satisfied customers will promote the company for free. Dissatisfied customers, in contrast, talk to far more people'. Again, 'Hell hath no fury like a dissatisfied customer.'

Pay full attention

If other matters, for example breaking off the conversation to take a telephone call, speaking to visitors, and so on, are allowed to interrupt the discussion the message 'Your complaint is not as important as these other matters' is conveyed to the customer. In such circumstances it is hardly surprising if aggravation and annoyance is generated.

Don't fidget

Yawning, fidgeting or glancing at a watch or clock shouts a hidden message to the other party, the message being 'This is a waste of my time, I'd sooner be elsewhere'. Whilst the latter might be the case, and even understandable, communicating this to the customer is not only rude but foolhardy as once again it can polarise attitudes and aggravate the whole situation.

Seat everyone

157

Aggression and aggressive behaviour is far more difficult to achieve when one is seated. The development of making the accommodation in football stadia all-seated results from awareness that the propensity to violence is reduced when people are seated. Thus, seating opponents should relax the parties and reduce the possibility of aggravation.

Serve refreshments

Whilst it will not always be possible or desirable to serve refreshments, the act has a dual advantage. Firstly, it is neutral and negative, yet creates a rapport by virtue of the shared experience. Secondly, the fact that the organisation is playing host may give it a slight edge in the rest of the encounter.

Be accountable

In the past it was often the case, particularly in contacting public sector and large private organisations, that the person responding would refuse to be identified. This shield of anonymity was frustrating to the caller for two reasons, firstly because it was an obvious way of avoiding any accountability, and secondly because, since the original contact was unknown, there was no way of ensuring a further conversation took place with a person conversant with the facts of the case. Fortunately this practice is fast disappearing. Effective complaint solution is best served by those responsible being identified by giving a name in letter and over the telephone, and by giving a name and having a name badge in face-to-face encounters.

Case study 13.2
Creating goodwill

The holiday company, when sending out a holiday itinerary which often had points that requiring checking or correction did not state a contact name. The holidaymaker suggested that a contact name be given. The company replied that it failed to see the point as the way it was set up, most of its staff could deal with any queries. The holidaymaker replied:

1 It's a pleasure business so formality is inappropriate.
2 It's a personal service business so a person's name is appropriate.
3 In giving a name you create rapport between customer and company
4 The business is very much of a 'repeat booking' type and providing a contact name will help create valuable bonds between customer and staff.
5 If problems arise, they may be more easily solved if such bonds exist than if the only contact is a reference number.

> **Key technique**
> Underlying these points is the need to prepare for problem incidence. If relationships, no matter how tenuous, have been created, particularly with long term, repeat customers, should problems arise, such rapport may be able to be exploited by the supplier in order to avoid, or at least minimise, demanding encounters. Creating good relationships in advance can create goodwill to be used when things are potentially more difficult.

Don't keep people waiting

Obviously this is difficult in the case of chance visitors, but even then there should be a minimum delay before he or she is seen. They should be invited to take a seat, provided with literature and possibly refreshments. Such courteous treatment may well aid a softening of any adversarial attitude. If an appointment is made, then, other than in the most extreme situation, the supplier should be there at the time stated. Keeping people waiting, particularly without apology or information merely stores up resentment that may find an outlet in a determination to be even more awkward than was hitherto the case. If there are delays then not only should an apology be made and an explanation offered, but also the customer should be given the choice of cancelling the appointment and setting another or waiting for a further stated time. Again, this is restoring choice to the customer to defuse difficult situations.

In addition, knowing the expected length of the delay can help.

Case study 13.3
Measured minutes

In recent years stations in the London underground system have been fitted with train indicators which, as well as showing the destination also display the length of waiting time. Whilst knowing how long one has to wait cannot reduce the delay, having the added information does seem to assist. The knowledge of the time before the train is due oddly enough 'seems' to make the wait shorter.

159

Always tell the truth

It is said that liars must have good memories – either that or they must take comprehensive notes. The trouble with telling lies is that they have a habit of backfiring as very often the truth comes out, which is very damaging to the instigator of the lie. In such circumstances any chance of a rapport or respect will have been lost and the likelihood of the dispute being settled amicably is dramatically reduced if not lost for good. The telling of lies is particularly aggravating to the recipient of the deception as he may feel that the organisation must regard him as a fool. Organisations that perceive their customers in this light can lose credibility. Thus, through lying, the clerk in case study 11.3 destroyed any sympathy he might otherwise have received from the customer whose initial approach was very much: 'Mistakes happen – just get it put right'. In trying either to cover up the mistake or the fact that he had not checked the position at all, the clerk was insulting the intelligence of the customer. This seriously backfired when the whole matter, including the lie, was reported to his superior. Not only was the reputation of the clerk destroyed it was yet another detraction from the reputation of a top UK bank. If the supplier was prepared to employ someone who could be caught in a silly and unnecessary lie, it is hardly a good reflection on the organisation itself. The fact that an organisation, through its employee, has lied is hardly a recommendation for consideration or placing repeat business with it, nor does it provide any confidence in future statements. Having said that, there are some organisations, for example some timeshare operators, who seem able to keep their operations going on a diet of lies and confidence tricks. Sadly they have not only defrauded their customers but have also brought into question the probity of the legitimate and 'straight' operators in that area of business.

160   Double dealing

Unfortunately, despite our best endeavours to deal openly, fairly and honestly with our customers and to ensure the 'dealing encounter' is conducted positively and to try to agree the problem swiftly without recourse to publicity or a third party or both, it has to be realised that some of our most demanding customers may not treat us in the same way. Inevitably, some customers will try to obtain recompense or restitution for what are no less than fraudulent reasons. Age is no barrier to these endeavours.

Case study 13.4
Sweet success

Some primary school children wrote to say how much they enjoyed the company's confectionery but had been disappointed by the range and quality of some of their favourite sweets. They sent back some samples which were found to be of poor quality, and the company responded by sending a supply of sweets of good quality with an apology.

Not only did they receive a nice letter of thanks, but also four or five more letters from other children in the same area trying out the same scheme!

Key technique

To avoid this 'toddlers sting', instead of sending some of the items referred to in the latest letters, the company sent samples of products which were not selling well, reasoning that:

- the children were after a free supply of their favourite sweet and responding positively could bring an avalanche of requests. However sending them an alternative might remove some of the attraction of the scam, whilst

- if the children liked the alternative it might generate more requests but might also generate more sales which could be beneficial.

Case study 13.5
Too much leeway

161

The newly appointed insurance manager was considering how strange it was that whenever one of the company vehicles was broken into, the employees' belongings stolen always seemed to be brand new – a new overcoat rather than an old anorak, a new leather briefcase rather than an old plastic one and so on. It was also odd that the sums involved always totalled around the maximum limit of the personal belongings cover. Then he discovered that the cover and its limit were referred to in the vehicle administration documents.

He removed the reference and sent out a memo advising all drivers that personal belongings would only be covered if they were kept in a locked boot whilst the driver was away from the car and should be covered under an individual's own household policy. The value of all such claims dropped considerably.

Sometimes the fact that a customer is so vociferous in pressing the complaint and for recompense, pays off. However, whilst there is no doubt that frustration from genuine loss can provoke honest anger, equally it does no harm to investigate all problems, since the shouting and threats may be being used as a kind of *legerdemain*, a device to distract attention from facts that would otherwise undermine the case being pressed.

Case study 13.6
'Methinks, she doth protest too much'

In October, several weeks after the agency had supplied an *au pair* to a family they informed the agency that the *au pair* was unsatisfactory as she had been stealing. In the circumstances, the agency agreed to find them a free replacement, even though under its terms it had no obligation to do so. The family stated that they did not want a replacement until the New Year and accordingly the agency made the necessary arrangements. Two days after the new *au pair* arrived in January the family rang the agency:

'This girl is absolutely useless.'

'I'm sorry to hear that – what's the problem?'

'She is useless around the house, dreadful with the children and she speaks hardly any English.'

'But that's why she has come to England – to learn the language, we said it was poor. I can't understand why she should have any difficulty with the children, she is the eldest of eight children and has plenty of experience.'

'I don't care about that – you have supplied someone who is no good at all to me – I want her replaced.'

'Don't you think you are being a little premature – after all it is quite an upheaval for a young girl to come to a foreign country and it takes time for her to settle down with a new family – don't you think you should give her a little time and help?'

'No – it's totally unacceptable – she's useless and so is your service – I want a replacement immediately.'

'But ...'

'Immediately do you hear, or I shall be taking this matter further.'

Key technique

Despite any vehemence facts must still be checked, not least to discover the reason for the vehemence. In this instance the agency discovered that the previous *au pair* had not been stealing, that she had been perfectly happy with the family and had not left them until just before Christmas and then only at their suggestion since they had a replacement coming in January! The family had concocted the story to avoid paying a fee for a replacement. However, since the replacement was not of the same calibre as the girl they had let go, their fury knew no bounds.

Fair game

Unfortunately the activities of some organisations lend themselves to customer abuse and even downright fraud so it is perhaps understandable if they are more cautious and less open when learning of details which might result in compensation, however classified. In recent years the abuse of the UK Social Services has been constantly featured in the media and the steps taken to ensure ever more rigorous scrutiny of claims and claimants is both understandable and to be welcomed by taxpayers. Whilst such scrutiny might not be appropriate in the context of the ordinary 'customers' referred to in this book, the checking process developed might bear copying. The Department of Social Security is reported as introducing a new system whereby claimants will be able to input personal details and details of their claim *via* an on-line interactive computerised touch screen presentation. Not only will claimants be guided through details of their claim but also, should they not understand a decision, the explanation can be repeated endlessly by the machine. Thus, as far as the staff are concerned, the frustration of many of such encounters should be reduced, whilst one assumes that being computerised the system will also be able to cross-check details of the claims in order to reduce the propensity to fraud to which the current system is susceptible.

163

Other organisations equally subjected to fraudulent claims are considering similar computerised systems.

Case study 13.7
A slippery customer

I started my business career with the Prudential Assurance company which owns or rents much of Holborn, London, around its chief office. Just after the second world war many old buildings (now replaced) were still standing. Some had cellars extending under the pavement which were partially lit by the use of pavement lights, or panels of iron into which were inserted a number of small squares of thick, part clear and part opaque glass. Unfortunately, whilst these were normally safe to walk on, they could be slippery when wet and dangerous, particularly if the glass became chipped or broken. A claim was received from an elderly man who had apparently slipped, fallen on a pavement light and dislocated his shoulder. The claim was processed and virtually completed when someone recalled that there had been a similar claim several months previously and cross-checked the details. It, and two or three others, were all found, despite the location of each accident being different, to feature someone who lived at the same address. Investigation proved that the claims were all made by the same man (using different names) who was able to dislocate his own shoulder!

Unfortunately insurance companies are often seen as 'fair game' by the unscrupulous and even those who consider themselves utterly honest discard such morals when completing an insurance claim form and either gild or falsify their claim. Insurance fraud is widespread and is running at an annual figure of around £400 000 000. To combat this, the insurance industry has invested in CLUE – a linked computerised system that will allow subscribers to cross-check information on all household insurance claims. Claimants will be computer screened and will be blacklisted, if found to have claimed fraudulently. Whilst the system will initially only record household insurance claims, investigations are under way to see if it can be extended to motor and other covers. Obviously having access to such a system should help reduce the incidence of 'demanding customers' dealing in such areas. The insurance industry may be wise to consider the introduction of the system with care since it in turn has a reputation for 'trying it on' with its policyholders, referring to print too small for most to read in their policies, whilst too many insurers have a reputation for being bad payers, regardless of the merits of a claim or the authority in the policy.

Bad payers

The UK recession of the early 1990s focussed the attention of many on a curiously British disease – that of debtors extending the terms of payment allowed them by suppliers. Chasing payment of invoices or amounts due has become a major problem for many UK suppliers leading to the launch, by the Confederation of British Industry, of a Code of Practice on Prompt Payment Practice, and, at the time of writing, a Department of Trade and Industry consultative document asking for input on proposals for government action to curb the delay of payment. Similar initiatives are being prepared for implementation throughout the European Union. Inevitably, business is only worth having if ultimately one is paid for the work. The operative word there is 'ultimately' since although most UK debtors do pay, they tend to extend the payment period considerably, illegally and with possible dire results to their creditor. The incidence of demanding encounters is high in this area, with the problems compounded by the creditor often being in the position of being unwilling to have recourse to legal sanctions as these may involve the loss of future business from the source. To try to reduce the incidence of such problems the suggestions set out in Figure 13.1 (a continuation of the 'Terms' checklist featured in Chapter 4) should be addressed.

CREDIT TO BE GRANTED ONLY ON AGREED TERMS

1 Ensure that terms and payment basis (strictly in accordance with terms of business) are shown clearly on quote/invoice.
2 Restrict size of orders until completion of [defined period] satisfactory trading/payment at lower levels.
3 Include retention of title clause in terms *.
4 Ensure payment terms are strictly adhered to, and that all customers know extensions of credit are not permitted.
5 If reciprocal trading takes place, stipulate that any debt owing by the business to the customer will be offset against any monies owed to the business by the customer *.
6 Charge interest on late payment *.
7 Recharge to customer any amounts levied by bankers for dealing with dishonoured cheques *.
8 Lay down strict procedures for guidance of credit control personnel, ensure adherence, and grant authority to threaten sanctions where necessary.
9 Credit control staff should be trained to be assertive, to chase for payment regularly and to visit awkward customers.
10 Ensure collection staff are trained to negotiate – and to bargain.
11 Stipulate that in the event of action being needed to be taken to recover debts, all costs incurred will also be due*.
12 Set up automatic procedure to action claims (i.e. *via* County Court etc.)

(Items marked * need to be incorporated in the terms of business, which themselves need to be written and widely promulgated.)

INVOICING AND CREDIT CONTROL

1 Invoices will be sent at the same time as delivery of goods/services or completion of orders. (Uncompleted orders should be avoided, since the non-completion of the order means the invoice cannot be served and the payment period cannot commence.)

---

2 Second class post will be used. (As the invoice will not be paid for over a month why pay for 'first class' service.)

3 Payment terms are end of month following invoice date (Every effort should be made to despatch orders with invoices before the end of each month.)

4 Payment terms can be extended by prior written authority of the Board only.

5 Seven days before the due date, a statement will be sent requesting prompt payment.

6 Two days after the due date, finance/credit control will check any reason for delay. If acceptable reasons are given set further time for chasing.

7 If an unacceptable reason is given for non-payment, a chasing letter (first class or faxed) sent stating that unless payment is made by return, the matter will be passed to solicitors and costs will be charged.

8 Two days later request solicitors to commence action. (There are a number of computerised packages for this purpose. These operate on a fail safe basis – i.e. they automatically generate the next stage of chasing unless action taken.)

9 Claim should include the original debt, costs of collection, including solicitors costs, plus interest on the amount due for the time overdue (which should be made clear in the terms – see above).

Key techniques

(1) If the customer knows when he will be invoiced, how this will happen and when the amount is due, his ability to evade due payment legitimately, and to generate confrontation is limited.

(2) Firm control over payment terms and the procedure, as well as regular chasing should aid recovery.

(3) Making notes of all that is said will build a file on the process, thus enabling the supplier to confirm or deny earlier statements.

Figure 13.1 'Getting the terms of business right' checklist

14

KISS and make up

Key learning points

1 Keeping the whole process as simple as possible will aid problem solution and avoidance.

2 Change can involve a propensity to make mistakes and cause customer complaints, thus it needs to be closely controlled.

3 The full effects of changes need to be thought through and planned for.

4 Using transactional analysis to determine the other party's responses given certain events can help achieve desired results.

5 Accepting that we can be in the wrong is essential.

6 Customer care is essentially about putting the customer's interests first and ensuring their requirements are met.

KISS

In this context KISS stands for 'keep it simple, stupid' and applies to a whole range of problems. It can be applied to customer care or complaint conversion since the concept is to try to ensure that explanations or interpretations, and thus negotiations or deals do not become bogged down in needless and convoluted language and discussion. The thrust of the argument is that if we keep the whole process and the wording and understanding, simple, then the scope for misunderstanding and imperfect recollection is considerably reduced. In addition, reducing matters to their simplest level, whilst avoiding any suggestion that one is patronising the other party should also reduce the time involved in the endeavour. After all, if the explanation cannot be misunderstood, further telephone calls or correspondence or discussion should be unnecessary. The parties can then move to the settlement stage. The more time spent in reconsidering matters, the more likely it is that a further edge could be discovered. If the deal is already done it becomes difficult to re-open negotiations. Often negotiations regarding customer complaints become unnecessarily complicated, resulting in positions becoming polarised, simply because too much time is allowed to pass on what can be called 'fencing' using statements and inferences all of which are capable of misinterpretation.

Case study 14.1
Why do they let it get that far?

Each week in the *Sunday Times*, Tony Hetherington deals with consumer complaints in a series of articles called 'Questions of cash'. Using the power of the press, publicity is given to examples of (usually) poor customer relations. Whilst in some cases the consumer has misunderstood the situation and the supplying company has an acceptable explanation, very often the impact of the column alone is sufficient to prompt supplying companies to compensate, negotiate or replace where previously they were refusing to do so. Since their names are quoted, publicity is given to their 'poor' customer relationships.

Very often positions become polarised, and the original complaint obscured, because the dispute has been allowed to drag on, in some cases for years rather than days or weeks.

Key techniques

(1) If the only way in which a customer can gain satisfaction is by using the power of the national press, it reflects badly on the way suppliers deal with demanding customers.

(2) Failing to foresee the potential adverse publicity is worse management than poor customer relations.

Remedial action

Place a time limit on the solution of customer disputes at set levels of managerial intervention. Referral to more senior levels of management, particularly where the latter are more able to see the global situation, and particularly the possibility of adverse publicity, may encourage earlier settlement or at least set in place a manner by which an internal solution can be found.

Managing change

Corporate complacency, which is a theme running through many of the disputes featured here and in the 'Questions of Cash' column, most of which could have been more satisfactorily resolved using negotiation techniques or even the Alternative Disputes Solution outlined in Chapter 9, is one of the most serious threats to avoiding and solving customer complaints. It is a dangerous conceit since the *status quo* exists only momentarily. If we are in the fortunate position of, for example, experiencing an excess of demand over productive capacity, experience should tell us that this will not last more than a few months or years at most. Exploiting our current strong position may be very attractive, but we ignore the possibility of the terms of trade swinging against us in the short to medium term. Everything changes constantly. If our organisations, our employees, our customers and our products did not change, it is likely that the number of difficult situations would be very low and continually reduce, as perfection of the *status quo* removes the possibility of mistakes being caused. However even in this unlikely scenario, change would still be going on around us. Materials, processes, market forces and social attitudes would still be changing which could lead us to situations where we would be forced to deal with the difficult if we have not kept pace with expectations. Realistically, we cannot stabilise even those matters under our control for very long. We must, therefore, accept as Cardinal Newman said that 'to change is to live', or in other words that change is endemic and unless we manage change we will never manage the demanding encounter. We should welcome change as a challenge to improve, recognising that it provides opportunities if well thought through. It is in initiating and responding to change with insufficient thought and planning, that we tend to create demanding encounters.

169

Case study 14.2
A left hand : right hand problem

The customer sent away to join a wine club and duly received his first case of wine. A few days later he received a letter from the club referring to the 'pack of information' contained in the case, as well as the vintage card, enclosed with the letter. He wrote to the club pointing out he had been sent neither. The response was a telephone call, which sought to explain that the vintage card was part of the membership card which had been enclosed with the letter. The customer patiently explained that the membership card he had received was a piece of plastic measuring about two inches by one inch and there was no vintage information on it. There was a pause and the supplier said 'Oh, I heard they were going to change to plastic membership cards, but I didn't think they had done it yet – I wonder what they're going to do about the vintage chart that was on the old membership card?'

'I really can't answer, isn't that your problem?' replied the customer quietly.

Key techniques

(1) This is a classic case where the effect of changes had not been fully thought through, or communicated to those who would have to relate to customers thereafter.

(2) Telephoning the customer was a sound tactic, particularly as the caller thought she would need to explain tactfully where to find the item, which could be difficult to achieve in writing without causing offence.

(3) Finally this is yet another example of the mistaken use of a standard letter. Despite the circumstances having changed the administration had not caught up. The supplier is trying to solve 1994's problem with 1993's administration – the only result can be the creation of demanding customers.

Case study 14.3
Change not to his liking

The family had holidayed in the UK seaside resort hotel for several years and had a good opinion of the value on offer. On one visit however, they found that not only had the price been increased considerably above the annual inflation figure, but also the service was nowhere near as good as hitherto, and nor was the quality or range of the food. In addition it seemed that insufficient attention was being paid to the real priorities of the facilities provided, even to the fact that unsafe practices were in operation.

At the end of the holiday the family were given a questionnaire asking for their comments on the hotel. Rather than completing the questionnaire, the holidaymaker wrote to the hotel owner pointing out the above and stating that, whilst he was not too worried about the price he paid, provided it was good value for the money, in this case the hotel seemed to have increased the price disproportionately whilst reducing the value it was giving.

A somewhat off-hand reply was received, which, reading between the lines, indicated to the holidaymaker that if he didn't like what was on offer for the price required, as far as the hotel was concerned, he could choose an alternative.

Two years later the hotel was in receivership.

> **Key technique**
> Whilst criticism might be safely resisted, particularly when the terms of trade are in our favour, we should never overlook the fact that the *status quo* is unlikely to be maintained for very long. Negotiation strength tends to run in cycles. Whereas at one time we might have a strong hand, it takes very little for such strength to be dissipated. The argument here arose towards the end of the UK boom of the 80's when demand was strong. In alienating some of its repeat-booking clients, the hotel lost some basic demand which would have been invaluable when the recession arrived but guests did not. Assuming demand will not be affected by changes outside our direct control is folly. Customer response should be framed with the realisation that terms of trade and demand do not remain constant. Long term demand and custom should never be taken for granted.

171

Implementing change

Human beings are essentially creatures of habit, and change can often be extraordinarily difficult to effect. There is an instinctive resistance to change, a fear of the unknown, which can be exacerbated by pride. To implement change we must plan the whole implementation and consider all the 'knock-on' effects. We must also be sure to communicate it to all involved. Not only is it essential that those who are involved know of the changes, but also in telling them we may generate consideration and communication of some effects we had not considered.

- keep those involved advised of on-going change and of changes to the changes, since even the most meticulously detailed plans tend to evolve in implementation

- generate enthusiasm for the changes, by involvement, explanation and reassurance

- monitor the introduction and initial operation of the changed system, procedure or other matter.

Case study 14.4
Not fully thought through

Under the Environment Protection Act 1990, only authorised waste con-tractors are legally able to remove and destroy non-domestic waste. Whilst in many industries the new act merely caused additional paper-work, in the medical profession it caused two real problems. Firstly chemists, who had formerly been able to dispose of surplus and unwanted drugs *via* hospital incinerators were no longer able to do so, as few hospitals registered as waste contractors, and thus many chemists accumulated a stock of unwanted drugs in store. Secondly, such drug stock posed a considerable attraction to addicts and others. Burglaries at chemists increased proportionately.

172

Key technique

The government is one organisation that can wash its hands of con-sideration of problems caused by its laws, but one would have thought the industry itself, in consideration of the implementation of the law would have given the matter advance consideration.

It may be difficult for senior management, responsible for such changes to imagine the real life position faced by their employees. Rather than developing paper or desk research-based guidance for use in such circumstances it may be preferable, when called in for training on the changes, to set up discussion periods during which a cross-section of problems experienced can be discussed with the aim of generating ideas for handling such situations from those who have experienced them first hand. Such brainstorming sessions can be very positive.

Case study 14.5
Up the pole

Pacific Power and Light is an American power supply company which operates in some rough conditions in the north-west USA. In many of the mountainous areas power is transmitted on overhead lines which often break under the weight of accumulated ice formed by the freezing of the constant snow. The method of avoiding breakages was to send linesmen along the line with poles constantly knocking the snow off before it froze. Several brainstorming sessions with the linesmen were held to try and solve this problem, during one of which a linesman complained that the previous week he had been chased by a bear. The suggestion was then made that if they could get the bears to climb the poles the weight of the animal would shake the snow off the lines, and another suggestion that if they put honey pots on top of the poles that would induce the bears to climb. The problem of how to place the honey pots on top of the pole then arose and the use of a helicopter was suggested. Cutting across this fanciful and increasingly risible idea came the notion that the downdraft from the helicopter rotors would itself remove the snow before it froze. Nowadays PP&L use the down draft from overflying helicopters to clear the lines.

173

Key technique

Perhaps only a few companies would have allowed a meeting of their staff, addressing the serious problem of change, to apparently go off on the fanciful tangent of encouraging bears to go after honey pots at the top of power poles, and yet it was only because they had gone through that idea that the eventual solution was discovered.

Diversification

Nowhere is there more danger of change giving rise to major problems than when the organisation diversifies. The incidence of problems and mistakes tends to be high when we are dealing with the unfamiliar. If the diversification results from the acquisition of a new part of the business, this can be exacerbated by our needing to induct new staff from the business in the way we want things done. Not only will the systems and procedures be alien to them, but also they may experience an unwillingness or reluctance to give up their old ways, or even a resistance and animosity to the newcomers, new systems and new ways of working. Very often such resistance, which will tend to create problems and difficult encounters, if allowed to exist unchecked, can be overcome by means of active communication with the employees concerned.

Case study 14.6
Care brings reward

When the Zodiac Toy chain acquired the Playbox 2000 and Youngsters Toy chains simultaneously every effort was made to make the staff of the 24 newly acquired shops feel that they constituted an important part of the enlarged chain, right from the start. A comprehensive folder of information about the company they had joined was produced and one was provided for every member of staff. In addition, on the day of acquisition every member of staff was seen both collectively and individually by a senior member of the acquiring company. As a result the acquisition went extremely smoothly, and several of the newly acquired shops featured among the weekly top ten sales shops of the whole chain. On-site briefings were undertaken and individual concerns explored immediately. Few real problems were experienced and the staff were quickly assimilated into, and became conversant with, the procedures of their new employer.

Conversely, several years later when Zodiac itself was taken over by different management, no such work or commitment was present, and a few months later the company went into receivership.

Case study 14.7
Trust brings reward

When the Laura Ashley chain had problems with some of its shops making losses, the company invited the staff of ten units to run the shops as they felt would be best. The results were impressive and one unit, at Liverpool, which had under-performed for a long time became the national number one store on a year on year increase in profits basis.

When things are running well and employees are motivated, the incidence of difficult encounters and demanding customers is likely to fall considerably. Conversely, when disturbing elements are at work, unless there is strong control, or respected corporate standards, difficult encounters can accumulate. In such circumstances, reassurance and reiteration of the basic needs and priorities is essential and must come from senior management, regardless of its other priorities.

Case study 14.8
Its a pleasure

Wishing to set a standard of employee, customer, neighbour and supplier and shareholder relationships, the Chairman devised the phrase 'It's a pleasure' and stipulated that it was to be a pleasure for all those with whom the company related to do business with the company. Considerable time was devoted to set up procedures and changing attitudes so that there was a real and practical effect to the adoption of the commitment embodied in the phrase. This extended to the retail units using the phrase whenever a customer said 'Thank you'. When subsequently a takeover bid was launched for the company, the Board was able to stress that during the bid it was essential that the commitment to all that was inherent in the use of the phrase should continue. Thanks to the preparatory work, during the nine weeks that the bid lasted, customer relationships were never higher and complaints never lower.

175

In the wrong

Very often it is our own attitudes and reactions that we have to change, and often there is nothing more difficult. For example, being prepared to acknowledge that one is in the wrong is impossible for some people and exceedingly difficult for others. One is reminded of the heartfelt plea of Oliver Cromwell when addressing the General Assembly of the Church of Scotland 'I beseech you, in the bowels of Christ, think it possible you might be mistaken', which might be a suitable slogan for all those required to deal with the demanding, whether they be opponent or ally. In facing difficult encounters the 'dealer' is faced with the problem of calculating and anticipating human response which is ever-changing. In this the onus for success lies with him, as he must react to the action taken by the customer. His/her initial actions and attitudes are crucial to the tone of the response and the success of the encounter. Although the initial tone may become conditioned by subsequent responses, the tone of the initial response will set the pattern for the rest of the exchange. If his attitude is negative and critical, then almost inevitably the instinctive response will be defensive and resentful, and there will be little chance of any rapport being created between the parties. Any negative approach will tend to create a negative response. Conversely, if the interview starts on a positive note, seeking rapport and understanding of the other party's views and problems, a positive response is far more likely, and the attainment of the desired result is more feasible. The inevitability of responses is set out in Figure 14.1.

If we live with criticism, we learn to condemn
If we live with hostility, we learn to fight
If we live with fear, we learn to be apprehensive
but
If we live with encouragement, we learn to be confident
If we live with praise, we learn to be appreciative
If we live with acceptance, we learn to respond

Figure 14.1 Generating responses (source unknown)

176 Appraising employees

Investing in people is all about training and developing employees so that they can do their jobs, and also the next job up, more effectively than previously, involving them in the organisation of the company and its development, and encouraging individuals to take greater responsibility. It parallells the movement to empower employees which is really only another phrase for thrusting authority and accountability as far down the chain of command as possible. Both ideas encompass the concept of making employees think of what they are doing, how they are doing it, and better ways of doing it, and are tailor-made criteria for those who interface with customers, since they, in turn, should be seeking to empower the customer, or restore the power of choice to a complainant. Employees' progress should be assessed regularly. Records of complaints and outcomes provide raw data, but discussion of problems and methods with senior management is also essential. For this reason regular appraisal of progress should be carried out. This seems obvious, and the need for performance checking has been referred to previously. However, research by Brunel University suggests that only around 10 per cent of companies include customer service in staff appraisals ('Service values, service deeds' Brunel University, Middlesex). If this is so it is perhaps hardly surprising if our performance in giving customer satisfaction is not well rated. Since 90 per cent of companies do not consider it necessary to check how well staff interface with customers, perhaps this indicates how low a regard many organisations have for the matter, in which case the incidence of complaint and subsequent poor rectification is hardly surprising.

Postscript

I completed this book in early February and in the following week the two incidents related below occurred. Nothing exemplifies better how to do it and how not to do it.

Case study 14.9
Getting it right

Four weeks before St. Valentines Day I ordered some flowers for delivery on 14th February from Marks & Spencer. Come the somewhat snowy day, the flowers did not arrive. At 6.30 p.m., on ringing the telesales desk, the young lady was extremely apologetic and, also genuinely sympathetic that the special delivery requested on that day had been missed. The flowers, delayed by the bad weather, were delivered the following day, but in compensation the company not only reimbursed the cost, but also within a week sent vouchers in excess of the cost, with a personal letter of apology.

177

Case study 14.10
How wrong can you get

The day the flowers arrived a household appliance on which we had taken out a service contract with the manufacturer developed a fault. On ringing the service number we were referred to another number with a different company and offered a visit five days later. The fact that our service contract (with the original company) promised a 48 hour call at a time to be designated by the customer 'including weekends' was brushed aside by the off-hand telesales staff, despite three phone calls trying to explain the contract terms. 'The computer does not recognise those terms – so it's Monday' was the only response. Eventually a message was left on an ansaphone offering a Saturday service provided we rang back to confirm we would be available at any time. On ringing back no-one knew anything about the Saturday offer and we were back to 'it's Monday or nothing'. Demanding to be put through to a more senior person, we initially fared no better – 'We've got you booked for Monday.'

Key techniques

(1) Callers were given only the telesales service telephone number. The operators would only refer to higher authority when threatened with legal action – in other words when, by their attitude, they had created an irate customer from a customer with a straightforward service requirement.

(2) No-one (even the more senior staff referred to) made any effort to take the details of the original contract which was obviously at variance with their standard contract, details of which were in their computer's memory.

(3) Having arranged a possible 'Saturday' appointment, the computer record had not been updated with a warning – essential when the customer was required to ring back, the supplier not having left a contact name.

(4) Not once was a word of apology offered by the operators.

Remedial actions

(1) Advise customers of any change of operator and seek approval of any change in terms. Terms cannot be changed unilaterally.

(2) Install adequate/computer records of the variations of service contract terms

(3) Train staff to be user-friendly and to say 'sorry' repeatedly in case of dispute. For 94 per cent of people, apology disarms complaint.

(4) Provide a careline for dissatisfied customers. Hiding behind anonymity only aggravates those determined to press their claim.

(5) When leaving a message provide a contact name for response. Using a real name creates a rapport with what can otherwise be a faceless organisation.

In the first case the problem was not the company's but nevertheless the company immediately accepted responsibility.

Result: a further enhancement of the company's reputation.

Everyone wins.

In the other case the problem was the company's but it refused to accept responsibility.

Result: referral of the matter to Board level, a full investigation and ultimately rectification all at the cost of a damaged reputation, considerable internal costs and dilution of management time.

Nobody wins.

Winning

Avoiding and dealing with demanding customers is essentially concerned with detail and getting it right first time. Customer and supplier form, or should form, a mutually dependent partnership. Only if this is the case and is **understood** by all involved to be the case will we both minimise the incident of complaints and be able to deal effectively with demanding encounters. Furthermore, it is not something which we can strive for and achieve once and then forget. It is ongoing and constant. It needs to be repetitive. It needs to form habits.

179

Bill Shankly, the manager of Liverpool Football club, which was during his managership the best team in the game, once said: 'when you get up you must have the intent to do the best you can that day, and the following day when you get up you have to have the intent to do the best you could that day, and so on'. Those that have to deal with customer complaints and problems need this kind of attitude as well as a realisation, which must and can only come from the top management of the company, that our businesses can only succeed to their full potential, and indeed may otherwise fail, if everyone has a commitment to:

- customer care and customer respect;
- providing service and response in the way we would like to be served and responded to;
- solving problems courteously, tactfully and swiftly, always bearing in mind that the best way of dealing with demanding customers is to avoid creating them in the first place.

Index

■